The Straight Pool Bible

The Straight Pool Bible

Personal Instruction from
a World Champion

Arthur "Babe" Cranfield
and Laurence S. Moy

The Lyons Press

Printed in Canada

10 9 8 7 6 5 4 3 2 1

Library of Congress Cataloging-in-Publication Data

Cranfield, Arthur.
    The straight pool bible : personal instruction from a world champion / Arthur "Babe" Cranfield and Laurence S. Moy.
        p. cm.
    Includes index.
    ISBN 1-58574-025-X
    1. Pool (Game)   I. Moy, Laurence S.   II. Title.

GV891.C742000
794.7'3—dc21

00-020307

With love and gratitude to our wives, Ruth Cranfield and Karen Chin Moy

14.1 Continuous [straight pool] is generally considered to be the game that provides the greatest all-around test of complete pocket-billiard playing skill, requiring great concentration, accuracy, shot-making, defense, patience and knowledge. It is the only commonly played game in which a shooter can play a single inning through rack after rack of balls. Players may shoot at any ball on the table at any time, but they must call the ball and the pocket on each shot. Unending variety . . . and challenge!

—The Billiard Congress
of America, *Official Rules
& Records Book*

Gee, you shoot straight pool, Mister?

—Paul Newman to
Jackie Gleason, *The Hustler*

Contents

Preface

I first met Babe Cranfield in 1978. He was 62 years old and I was an 18-year-old freshman at Cornell University in Ithaca, New York. At least once each year, Babe would make the one-hour drive from his home in Syracuse, New York, to Ithaca to give an exhibition at Cornell. As part of his exhibition, Babe would play whoever had won the local tournament. This gave me the chance to play him a number of times. And since I went on to Cornell Law School, I had the privilege of being humiliated by Babe in straight pool matches over seven years.

Babe displayed his generosity to me early on. After we played for the first time, he told me I could call him up and arrange to meet him in Syracuse for a pool lesson. Before my first lesson, I made a trip to the bank to withdraw $100—a significant chunk of my college-student finances. My custom-made cue, which Danny Janes of Joss Cues had just sent to me, cost only $165 and came with two shafts with ivory ferrules! Still, I had no idea how much a pool lesson with a world champion was supposed to cost. I only hoped that $100 would be enough.

Babe and I met at a place called the Holiday Bowl, a huge bowling and billiards center that no longer exists. Babe spent nearly two hours with me, explaining aspects of the game that no one had ever taken the trouble to teach to me. He got his ideas across in a direct and simple way. His words showed that he understood an incredible amount about the most complex aspects of pool. He was uncanny at expressing himself and describing what I had to accomplish on the table to improve. Most of what I had learned up to that point had been learned the hard way: from matching up with older, more experienced players in the poolroom near my home, watching other players, reading the few books in print at that time, and trial and error.

As we walked to the cash register at the front desk, I asked Babe how much I owed him for the lesson. He told me, "Don't worry about it. Just practice what I told you, and give me a call in five or six weeks after you're ready to come up again." That was the start of my friendship with Arthur "Babe" Cranfield Jr.

Babe's story obviously began long before that.

Arthur E. Cranfield Jr. got his nickname as a kid in the poolroom his father owned near Yankee Stadium. Babe Ruth, the ballplayer, used to stop by from time to time. Cranfield pestered Ruth for tickets to Yankee games, but didn't end up going to them. There was a Chinese restaurant next door to the poolroom, and Cranfield used to trade baseball tickets for food with a kid who worked in the kitchen. Eventually, Ruth caught on to Cranfield's scam. To his credit, however, Ruth wasn't upset when he found out he'd been used; he just wanted his fair share of the food! From that point on the young Art Cranfield and Babe Ruth went partners . . . and Babe Cranfield had a new nickname.

Babe Cranfield was a true prodigy. He gave pool exhibitions while still in grade school and, by age 12, was running 100s in straight pool. In the 1920s and 1930s running a 100 was much more difficult than it is now due to the difficult playing conditions of that era, including inferior rails and balls and smaller pockets.

Babe became a consistent champion at pool. As a 15-year-old he won the U.S. Junior Championship. Then he moved on to senior competition, where he captured the U.S. Amateur title on his first attempt. Babe ended up winning that championship a total of three times, in 1938, 1939, and 1940. When he won the Amateurs for the first time, he was the youngest person to do so, at age 22.

Babe's biggest win was the World's Professional Championship. In the 1964 World's Professional tournament, he played well, finishing second. Along the way, he ran 141 while defeating Irving Crane by the score of 150 to -2. By placing second to Luther Lassiter, Babe earned the right to challenge Lassiter for the championship, which he did that same year.

Although Babe was the underdog in the title match and Lassiter had the support of nearly all of the crowd, the final score was Babe Cranfield 1,200, Luther Lassiter 730. Two amazing things happened during this title match. One was that Babe called a foul on himself that not even the referee, Cue Ball Kelly, or Lassiter had seen—which tells you something about the character of Babe Cranfield. The other was that Babe put Lassiter into such a state with his constant pounding that at one point, Lassiter picked up the cue ball after Babe had finished shooting, thinking Babe had scratched when he hadn't. Perhaps equally amazing, Babe was able to compete at the highest level of play and *succeed* at the same time he was working full time as a vice president for a Muzak distributor. The fact that Babe was able to accomplish so much without the luxury that most players enjoyed—devoting himself exclusively to billiards—is truly remarkable.

Once Babe won the World's Professional Championship, he made history. He became the only person to win the highest titles available at every possible level: junior, amateur, and professional. No one—before or since—has accomplished this feat.

Beyond these competitive achievements, through more than 2,000 exhibitions, Babe has brought the sport to many, many people. This is no surprise given his generous spirit and his reputation as the thinking man's pool player. I still remember the very first exhibition that I saw him perform. When he finished, people literally *ran* to him to find out more about this fascinating game, which they had never seen played before, at least not at Babe's level. And these new fans didn't hear Babe brag about how great he was to master such a difficult sport. Instead, he told them how simple the game is, and how they could enjoy it immediately with just a little practice.

Through studying billiards, competing, winning, and teaching, Babe Cranfield has been an important part of the game over most of the 20th century. In recognition of all that Babe has given to the game, the Billiard Congress of America (BCA) awarded him its highest honor, induction into its Hall of Fame, on July 19, 1997. As one of pool's grandmasters, Babe has always had a great deal to offer students of the game.

Today Babe no longer performs exhibitions. Despite a stroke that has left him with impaired eyesight, however, he still helps people learn the game. As he demonstrated by his willingness to spend two hours explaining the principles of pool to me, a near stranger, 21 years ago, Babe has always been willing to work with anyone interested in learning, no matter what his or her ability level. Beginning with that first lesson, Babe improved my game. He'll do the same for you.

Larry Moy

Introduction

When you reach the age of 84, there are times when you consider your life's work. I devoted much of my life to straight pool. Even while just practicing alone, I loved the complex simplicity of straight pool. It's an easy game in terms of understanding the objective: Get any ball into any pocket. But it can seem awfully hard at times. Straight pool is not like nineball, where the numbers on the balls dictate your shot selection. Instead you get to play any object ball on the table. This might seem easier initially, but it requires you to impose your vision of how to run out a table upon a random array of balls. To succeed at straight pool, you must instill order upon chaos. You've got to think and react on your feet. You also have to execute—that is, make your shots. The whole mix is intoxicating for me.

As great a game as straight pool is, it has had its ups and downs in terms of popularity, not unlike pool generally. At different times in my life, I have been treated like a celebrity and shunned as a pool bum. Without question, billiards has allowed me—indeed, *required* me—to view the highest heights and deepest depths from the same perch. Unlike the popularity of pool, however, some things have not changed. The game of straight pool remains the wonderful challenge that it has always been. The game and the experiences that come with playing it have profoundly educated me, and now I'd like to share some of what I've learned about the game I love.

Whether you know it yet or not, straight pool is the ultimate test of billiards intellect and ability. Straight pool strikes a balance between the shot-making emphasized by nine-ball, on the one hand, and the strategic knowledge (or moves) stressed by one-pocket, on the other. The outcome of a nine-ball match so often seems to turn on who gets the good rolls and who gets the bad ones—a euphemism for luck. Not so with straight pool, especially not over a long match such as the block competitions featured in years past (playing to a total of 1,000 or more points over several days in segments or "blocks" of 200).

Although nine-ball now dominates the billiards scene, it's my hope and aim that the following chapters, which focus on straight pool, will prove instructive for all players. I have never seen a solid straight pool player who could not learn to play any of the other games well if he or she had the interest. Much of what straight pool teaches—minimizing cue ball movement, for example—applies also to nine-ball, at least to some extent. You will, for example, certainly be required to move the cue ball more in a nine-ball game than in a straight pool game. All other things being equal, however, the nine-ball player who can keep cue ball movement to the minimum possible *under the circumstances* will win. Straight pool teaches this economy.

I hope that—whatever game you play—you play better after reading what I am about to share with you.

Babe Cranfield

The Game

The rules of straight pool are simple. All 15 object balls are used, and a player earns 1 point for each called shot pocketed. When all but the last ball of the rack have been made, the cue ball and the object ball are left where they lie, and the remaining 14 are reracked, with the apex spot left empty. The next shot is the break shot. The player strives to pocket the break ball and, in the same shot, drive the cue ball into the rack of 14 to separate the balls so that new shots are created and his or her run can continue. (This is why the game is also known as "14.1 Continuous.") The game is won when one of the players reaches a designated number of points, usually 150 or more for professionals. Less experienced players often play to 50 or 75 points.

Even the very first shot of a straight pool game must be called. For this reason, the standard opening shot is a safety. On this opening safety, at least two object balls and the cue ball must touch a rail after the cue ball contacts the rack. The standard opening safety is to graze one of the ends of the bottom row of balls, driving the balls at each end of the bottom row to a rail while sending the cue ball to the bottom rail, to the side rail, and then back up to the head of the table. After the opening safety, a player has made a legal shot so long as he or she contacts an object ball with the cue ball and then either pockets a ball or contacts a rail with the cue ball or an object ball. If a player fouls (either by failing to execute a legal shot or by scratching the cue ball into a pocket) three times in a row, he or she is penalized 15 points or more, depending upon the length of the game.

Given the rules of straight pool, the game offers the theoretical possibility of running an infinite number of balls. When straight pool was the game played in every major tournament and determined the world champion, straight pool was known as the "Championship Game." During this period of straight pool dominance, nearly every professional had run at least 100 balls at one time or another. Some were capable of running several hundred without a miss. Today, although most pros are certainly capable of running 100, some have not had enough exposure to straight pool to test whether that is true in their particular case.

At any level of straight pool, much depends on whether a player is able to set up for good break shots. The last several shots in any given frame before the break shot are thus critical. For this reason, the ball to be played immediately before the break ball is called the key ball.

If, at the end of a frame, the break ball ends up within the rack area, the break ball is spotted at the head spot and the cue ball remains where it lies. If both break ball and cue ball are in the rack area, all 15 balls are racked and the incoming player can place the cue ball anywhere behind the head string (the line that intersects the head spot). If the cue ball is in the rack area and the break ball is outside the rack area but below the head string, the cue ball may be placed anywhere behind the head string and the break ball remains where it lies.

The
Straight
Pool Bible

CHAPTER

Equipment

I was 22 years old when an enterprising fellow named Sylvester Livingston booked me for my first cross-country exhibition tour. The deal included free use of a car and $110 a week, which was a good deal at the time: In 1938, entire families were getting by on a lot less. I played two to four exhibitions (which included matches against the local hero) a day. From the road, I'd call home to talk to my parents. My dad, Arthur Cranfield Sr., was an accomplished athlete (he gave me my interest in nearly everything—billiards, golf, baseball, tennis, bowling, basketball . . .), trained boxers, and owned a billiard room at the time. I'd tell him about how I had to play on a slow 5- by 10-foot table in the morning, then drive 200 miles and switch over to a fast 4½- by 9-foot table that same afternoon, and the like. (Once I had to give my exhibition on a snooker table!) My dad thought it was healthy; he called it part of the "hardening process."

Tables

Most chapters on billiards equipment begin with a discussion of selecting a cue. Before I reach that subject, I'd like to say a word about selecting a table. By that I do not mean how to buy a table, but rather how to select one in a commercial poolroom for practice.

While I have been offered tables for free, and my home could probably accommodate one, I have always refused. Playing under varying conditions develops a touch and sensitivity that you'll never duplicate by using the same table over and over again. If buying a table will allow you to practice more, then by all means do so. But whether or not you own a table, when you're practicing in a commercial room, make a point of choosing a different table on each occasion you play. You will avoid consciously and subconsciously relying upon conditions that are likely to differ when you are competing.

Every time you try a new table, test how it plays. Shoot at slow speeds into each pocket from several angles to find out if the table rolls left or right in certain spots. Shoot balls down each of the rails to see whether the table will keep the ball on a straight path all the way to the pocket. Bank balls off each rail to learn whether it banks long (creating a wider angle than expected), short (creating a narrower angle than expected), or neither.

Under ideal conditions, many of us can play well. Champions, however, always seem to be able to adapt to whatever a table offers, although they usually play under the best conditions. Part of this ability comes from preparation—checking the table thoroughly and observing carefully all of its characteristics. The rest comes from being able to make the necessary adjustments. For example, if you discover that a particular rail banks short, you can then hit your banks against that rail with less speed to widen the angle. Or if you notice that a particular table rolls less than perfectly but is only slightly off, you'll want to avoid hitting shots softly, moving the cue ball with a firmer stroke rather than rolling the cue ball for position.

When testing a table you must, above all else, gauge its speed. As almost everyone knows, newer cloth plays faster. So does cloth that is extremely worn. Different brands of cloth play at different speeds, and, to make matters worse, different parts of the same table (including the cushions) may play at all different speeds. Countless games have been won or lost based on a failure to adjust to the speed of the table. Do not count on figuring out this speed as your game or match progresses. Instead, take the time to develop a feel for it before beginning your match.

I believe that when a player is said to have gotten into a zone—to be completely "in stroke"—much of what is occurring is what I have tried to describe in the above paragraphs. Incredibly, part of the "dead-stroke" phenomenon—where everything is easy and the player simply cannot miss—comes down to such mundane acts as reading a table's speed and adjusting to it. Learn to do this and you will never feel awkward on a strange or new table again.

Cues

On to cues. I play with the same Rambow cue that I've used for over 60 years. At the time I began to use it, Herman Rambow and one or two other cue makers stood out as people who built reliable instruments. The challenge for cue makers at that time, as now, was to make a two-piece, jointed cue that hit as solidly as one piece of wood. Back then, if you wanted a jointed cue that played as well as a one-piece, you probably went to Mr. Rambow. (Rambow made a shorter-than-standard-length cue for me when I was a junior competitor. I eventually graduated to a full-length cue and became comfortable with a weight of between 19 and 20 ounces, along with a 12¾-millimeter tip diameter. My cue is 57 inches in length.)

Today many manufacturers and individual crafts-men make perfectly good cues, and, unless you're in-vesting in cues or want something decorative for the sake of looks alone, there is no need to buy a fancy model. Fancier cues do not play any better than plain ones. If you like the playing characteristics of cues pro-duced by a particular cue maker, it may be possible for you to afford the cue you want (even from one of the more expensive makers) if you avoid excessive orna-mentation. (Some cue makers believe that the greater the number and size of decorative inlays on a cue, the *worse* that cue will play, since these inserts require more spaces to be drilled out of its chassis.)

The key is to find something you're comfortable with and stay with it so that it becomes even more com-fortable. In that way, your abilities to develop a feel for the cue ball and to make fine adjustments in how you address it can be enhanced.

In contrast to my advice on tables, I do recommend that you purchase your own cue if you plan to take up the game seriously. Before you buy, try as many differ-ent types of cues as possible. By the time you're ready to invest in your own, you'll know whether you prefer a metal, plastic, or ivory joint; a linen or a leather wrap; an ivory, fiber, or plastic ferrule; and the like.

The most important part of a cue is the tip. Whether you are picking a house cue off the rack or buying a one-of-a-kind handcrafted stick, make sure that it has a good tip. The tip should be hard enough to sustain its shape. That way, once you've shaped the tip evenly all the way around, you can count on it to contact the cue ball in a consistent manner. For most players, the harder the tip, the better. Test a tip for hardness by pressing it with your fingernail. If the tip is not yet on the cue, you can simply bite on it to find out if it has the correct hardness.

How you hit the cue ball affects the tip shape. For example, if you generally stroke the ball at or near the center (a good trait, incidentally), the tip of your cue will naturally wear down differently from that of someone who often loads up shots with english. The latter player's tip will naturally wear to a higher—that is, steeper—crown. If you want your tip to maintain its shape, don't let other players use your cue for any length of time.

Cases

Once you've found a cue you like, invest in a good case. I prefer a hard case, which protects against more hazards than a soft one, even though carrying a hard case adds weight. Also, with a hard case it's easier to stand the cue straight up when it's in storage, which makes it less likely that your cue will warp.

Pocket Billiard Balls

When I toured for exhibitions, I always brought along my own pocket billiard balls, which are Brunswick Centennials. (The balls I use to this day are one of the two sets of Centennial balls that Luther Lassiter and I used during our 1964 challenge match for the World's Professional title. I donated the other set to a charity auction several years ago.) These days many of the upscale commercial rooms use only high-quality balls. You can tell whether a ball is high quality by spinning it and checking for roundness. If the ball is close to perfectly round, it looks as if it's still even while it's spinning, with no hint of wobbling. Also, the finish of a better-quality ball is generally shinier than that of an inferior ball, and the numbers and other markings show clean and consistent lines.

If the room you visit does not provide a suitable rack of balls (or, worse still, hands out racks of balls that are mixed and matched from several different sets made by different manufacturers, which you can detect from the styling of the numbers), go somewhere else. At least find out whether the house keeps a few better sets of balls for its regular customers.

CHAPTER

Learning to Learn

I was on the road, playing in Philadelphia. During the day I played in an open golf tournament, and at night I'd play pool. I considered turning pro in golf but never took that step, although I did win some titles as an amateur. One of the pros playing in the open tourney in Philadelphia that year was Ben Hogan. After finishing a round, I was practicing drives off the tee. Hogan saw this and said: "What the hell are you doing practicing drives? You were hitting your drives great all day, but I saw you having trouble getting out of the traps. Get your butt over to those sand traps!"

This was the single most important pool lesson I ever got: Practice your weaknesses, not your strengths.

You will never be able to improve upon your natural ability. Neither will I. No matter what you start out with, however, you can improve your game.

Focus

Some of this is mental attitude and personality. Ralph Greenleaf was obviously talented (perhaps the game's *most* talented champion), but he also found a way to play better against better players. Jimmy Caras, another world champion, had a similar ability. There was something in Jimmy's makeup that needed to win and refused to give up. I strongly believe that you can improve your mental attitude, a subject I'll address in more detail in chapter 10.

Practice

Another part of improving is practice. I won't expand on the story that starts this chapter other than to say that most players could use work on playing shots off the rail, bridging over balls, shooting with the opposite hand, and stroking comfortably while using reverse english. Shooting with the opposite hand is a critical skill; just look at how many shots (or efforts to obtain proper position) are missed when a player picks up the mechanical bridge because using it requires an entirely different motion from his or her usual stroke. Even professionals, who generally excel at all aspects of play, exhibit weaknesses in particular parts of their games. Those who can address these deficiencies will necessarily become even more formidable.

What can you do to improve? Learn from your errors. You must start by disciplining yourself to become completely aware of what is happening on the table. When you miss, observe which side of the pocket you missed on. Did the cue ball roll too far or not far enough on your last effort to play position? Do you tend to miss break shots? Do you make them but end up without a shot?

You don't need to dwell on the negative. Adopt a positive mental attitude, but be aware enough of what's going on (and honest enough with yourself) to pick up these clues when something does go awry. In that way, you can improve as your match wears on.

Watch Your Opponent

For that matter, you can pick up a lot from watching your opponent. The speed of the table and whether the rails bank long or short can be observed. Also, you can find out whether a particular pocket is tight or easy, giving you information you can use when your turn at the table arrives. All of this can—and should—be picked up by remaining mentally focused on the game throughout, even when you are sitting down.

Watching your opponent carries other bonuses. After an opponent misses or attempts a safety, he or she will often let on (through facial expression or body language) that a combination or a carom is dead on, or that a shot can squeak by other balls to the pocket. Watch your opponent to see what he or she is watching. Does he or she avoid certain types of shots? Does your opponent appear uncomfortable shooting particular shots (such as long shots, cut shots, straight-in shots, shots off the rail, shots requiring a bridge to be made over a ball)? All of these factors should influence your choices regarding how to play safeties against your opponent. This information is particularly useful in a nine-ball game, where you have the option to "push out" and challenge your opponent to attempt a shot or a safety immediately after the break.

Teach

Another way to learn is by teaching. Many times, requiring yourself to describe a certain technique or particular effect improves your own understanding and awareness. It's a mutually beneficial situation. And in any case the game of pocket billiards is worth sharing.

Pocketing Balls

Most players make pocketing balls tougher than it needs to be. Pocketing balls should be simple. Kids seem to have an easy time of it. Seasoned players often have more trouble pocketing balls after playing a few years than they did when they first started out. (The need to play position is not a complete explanation of this phenomenon, since advanced players and beginners alike should be playing most shots with little or no english.)

This chapter addresses the most fundamental aspect of maintaining a straight pool run: making your shots. Even the most advanced players often face the end of a multi-rack run due to a miss on a makable ball. The way to avoid missing is to simplify your aiming process. More accurately, *don't complicate it.* I'll begin by revisiting the basics of aiming, something that is helpful to players of every level of skill.

Three Straight Lines

Making a shot involves three straight lines. The first line is the cue, so you initially need to focus yourself only on the two remaining lines: the desired line from the cue ball to the object ball, and the desired line from the object ball to the pocket. See illustration 1.

Figuring out where to aim the cue ball is the first step. Once you do that, the other lines fall into place.

An important fundamental truth is that the point at which you aim the cue ball is nearly always different from the point where the cue ball and object ball make contact. The only time the point of aim and the point of contact are the same is when your shot is straight into the pocket. See illustration 2.

On thin cut shots—shots where the cue ball contacts the edge of the object ball (in contrast to shots that are straight or nearly straight in), the point of aim is significantly away from the object ball. See illustration 3.

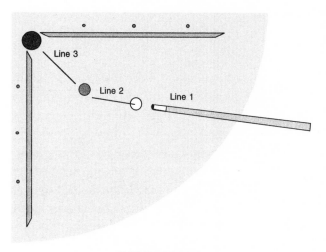

ILLUSTRATION 1

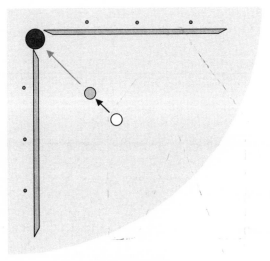

ILLUSTRATION 2

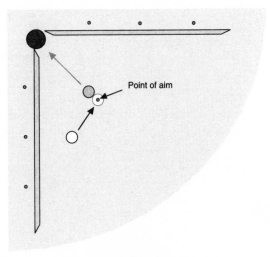

Point of aim

ILLUSTRATION 3

Once you properly visualize the point of aim, executing a thin cut shot isn't much different from executing a straight-in shot. In both cases the cue ball must be in the absolutely correct place at the time it contacts the object ball for the object ball to go in. If the cue ball makes contact at the proper point, the object ball *must go in.* If, on the other hand, the cue ball makes contact at any other point, the shot will never work. It's important that you visualize the aiming point that allows the cue ball to contact the correct point on the object ball. Once you do that, all you need to do is deliver the cue ball to the point of aim—that is, make sure line 1 (your cue) and line 2 (the desired path of the cue ball) are aligned when you execute the shot.

Maintaining Your Rhythm

Do not allow the pace of your shot-making to be dictated by how easy or difficult a shot appears to be. Whether you are shooting a short straight-in shot or a nearly 90-degree cut shot, take whatever time is necessary to visualize the precise point where you must aim the cue ball. Even when you're faced with a short or relatively straight shot, wait until you've precisely visualized the point of aim before you pull the trigger. If you are having trouble visualizing the shot, stand up and begin again. Even on short- and medium-length straight-in shots, the object ball must be contacted at the proper point. Many straight and nearly straight shots are missed when a player does not take the same care he or she would use for other, more angled, shots.

Similarly, do not unnecessarily dwell on a shot just because it's a thin cut shot. If you have visualized the precise point of aim, take the same number of practice strokes you routinely take and then execute the shot. You will find that by adopting the rhythm you use on all your shots for your thin cut shots, you will pocket more of them. Your confidence in playing such shots will grow, and you will no longer feel the need to take an excessive amount of time on them.

The Arrow

Some years ago I developed an aiming tool that I call, simply, the Arrow. This device has been useful to me when I've fallen into patterns of having difficulty seeing the correct point of aim. The Arrow is particularly helpful to newer players, who need to train their eye to aim the cue ball at a point off the object ball in order to pocket thin cut shots. You can also use the Arrow to learn to visualize caroms (or billiards), which I'll discuss later in this chapter; they're depicted in illustrations 8 and 9.

An actual-size drawing of the Arrow is found at illustration 4. Use that drawing to fashion your own Arrow out of thin cardboard (such as an index card or business card) or thin plastic.

Note the dimensions of the Arrow. A regulation pocket billiard ball measures 2¼ inches in diameter. The full length of the Arrow is also exactly 2¼ inches. The distance from the end of the Arrow to the tip of the interior point is 1⅛ inches, half the diameter of a ball. The distance from the tip of the interior point to the tip of the exterior point is also 1⅛ inches. These dimensions are what allow the Arrow to work.

For any shot anywhere on the table, place the arrow so that it's lined up with the intended pocket and its in-

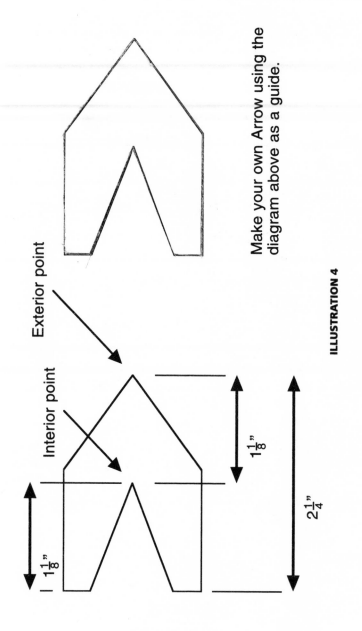

Make your own Arrow using the diagram above as a guide.

Exterior point

Interior point

$1\frac{1}{8}$"

$2\frac{1}{4}$"

$1\frac{1}{8}$"

ILLUSTRATION 4

terior point is directly under the edge of the object ball, at the precise point where the cue ball must contact the object ball for the shot to be made. See illustration 5. The exterior point is now *exactly half a ball's width away.* This exterior point is the *aiming* point—that is, the point at which you aim the center of the cue ball.

If you are able to deliver the cue ball so that it rolls over the exterior point of the arrow, the cue ball must contact the object ball at the proper contact point, and the object ball must go in. *This is true no matter where the cue ball is located at the start of the shot.* See illustration 6. Being aware of this fact takes some of the mystique out

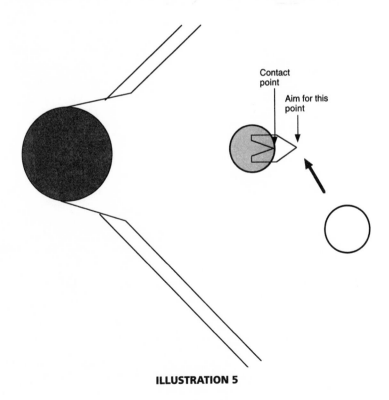

ILLUSTRATION 5

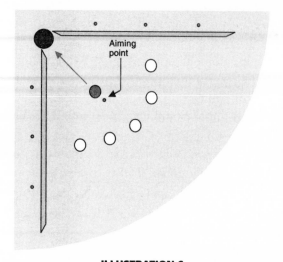

ILLUSTRATION 6

The aiming point never changes, irrespective of where the cue ball is located.

of pocketing balls. Since the point of contact never changes, every shot you see—in a sense—is exactly like the one you just played.

Everyone has trouble visualizing particular types of shots. Practicing these uncomfortable shots five to fifteen times with the Arrow helps program your eyes and brain to correctly see such shots. You will become more comfortable and will be able to locate the aiming and contact points more easily in a game.

In a game situation (when, of course, you're aiming without using the Arrow), always look at each shot from the straight-in perspective. In other words, examine the object ball from the vantage point directly opposite the pocket. See illustration 7. No matter how advanced you are, this simple routine will reduce misses.

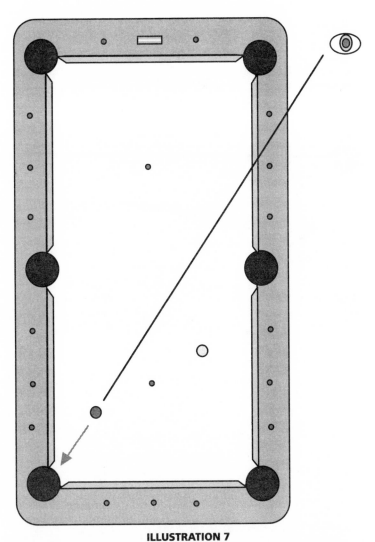

ILLUSTRATION 7

Always study every shot from this vantage point (directly opposite the pocket) to help pinpoint the correct point of contact and visualize the correct point of aim.

Caroms

For most angled shots where the cue ball and object ball are fairly close together, a cue ball struck at its center (a center-ball hit) will travel away from an object ball along the tangent line after contact. The tangent line runs perpendicular to the line connecting the center of the cue ball and the center of the object ball at the moment of impact. See illustration 8. The same is true for longer

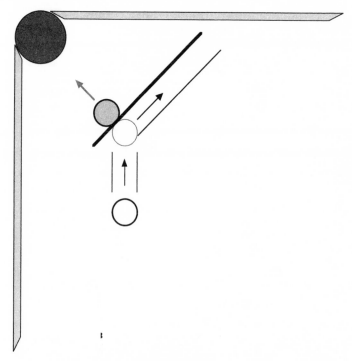

ILLUSTRATION 8

The cue ball, after contacting the object ball, travels along the tangent line (the bold line in this illustration). This rule holds true so long as the cue ball has neither forward roll (follow) nor reverse spin (draw) at the moment of contact.

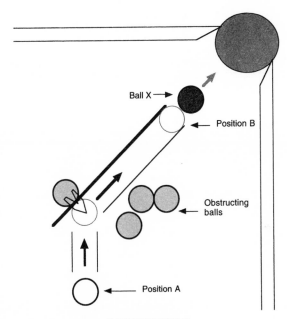

Ball X →

Position B →

Obstructing balls →

Position A →

ILLUSTRATION 9
Playing a Billiard Using the Arrow
The cue ball lies at position A, leaving no clear shot to pocket the black ball, ball X, due to the obstructing balls. To make ball X, the cue ball must end up at position B, meaning that the desired tangent line is as shown. (The desired tangent line is the bold line.)

Place the Arrow with the interior point at the edge of the first object ball, at a 90-degree angle to the tangent. Then, like any other shot, simply aim at the exterior point of the Arrow.

shots, so long as—at the time the cue ball is contacting the object ball—the cue ball has neither draw nor follow. Visualizing caroms (sometimes called billiards) comes with practice and experience, just like any other aspect of the game. The Arrow can help speed up that process.

Place the Arrow so that it lies at a 90-degree angle to the desired tangent line, with the interior point of the Arrow at the edge of the first object ball. See illustration

9. Once that is done, aim the center of the cue ball at the exterior point of the Arrow to make the billiard.

I'm sure you will find your own applications for this aiming tool. To give you an idea how much importance I place on the Arrow, I seriously considered focusing this entire book on aiming with the Arrow. It can teach new players, and remind experienced ones, how to aim the cue ball. I have never found a device or system that works better for me or my students.

English

English is a necessary evil. It's necessary because sometimes you simply cannot execute a shot and obtain good results without it. There exists a temptation, however, to use english more than necessary (sometimes to the point where you apply it out of habit). This causes players of all levels to miss shots and position far more often than they should.

People define *english* differently. My own definition is, "the spin imparted to the cue ball when it is struck to the left or right of center." Some people define the term to also include hitting with draw (stroking the cue ball below center to cause it to spin backward) and hitting the cue ball with follow (stroking the cue ball above center to give it extra forward rotation). As every player knows, hitting the cue ball to the right of center—right english—causes the cue ball to curve to the right, since it is spinning from left to right. Stroking the cue ball to the left of center causes it to curve to the left.

Although english is a vital tool, keep in mind at all times that most shots can be made with very little english, or none at all. In many situations you can both pocket the desired object ball and position the cue ball for your next shot using only stop, follow, or draw.

When you do apply english, it's best to avoid stroking the cue ball too far away from the vertical-center axis, or centerline. Ideally, you will play the vast majority of your shots keeping the tip of the cue stick within one cue tip's width of the centerline. See illustration 10. Stroking too far from center causes miscues and complicates the aiming process by causing severe "squirt". Squirt occurs when, due to the application of english, the cue ball initially moves in the opposite direction from the one in which you struck the cue ball. For example, if you are applying heavy right-hand english, the cue ball will first move to the left. At some point, however, the spin applied to the cue ball will curve it to the right. You must somehow judge how these effects will require you to adjust your aiming point. This will depend upon how much english is applied, the speed of the stroke, the distance between the

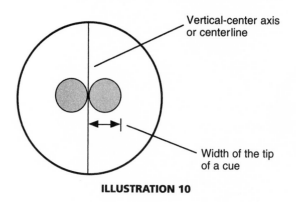

Vertical-center axis
or centerline

Width of the tip
of a cue

ILLUSTRATION 10

cue ball and the object ball, and the characteristics of your particular stroke (different players obtain different amounts of spin even when they strike the cue ball the same distance from its center). This is easier said than done—a good reason to avoid excessive english.

To make sure we are speaking the same language, let me define some additional terms.

Outside versus Inside English

Outside english means that you are applying english on the side of the cue ball opposite the direction in which you are cutting the object ball. Thus, in illustration 11, the object ball is being cut to the left in order to pocket the ball. In this case, outside english is right english. Obviously, then, inside english is applied when you are

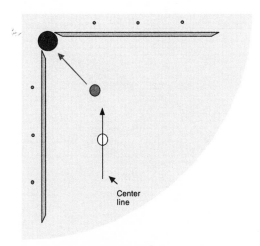

ILLUSTRATION 11

In this example, applying inside english would involve stroking the cue ball to the left of the centerline.

Stroking the cue ball to the right of the centerline, in this example, applies outside english.

stroking the cue ball on the same side as the direction in which you are cutting the object ball. Looking at illustration 11 once again: Since the object ball is being cut to the left, inside english is left english.

Running English versus Reverse English

Running english also describes which side of the cue ball is being struck, but the term is defined by how the cue ball reacts when it strikes a rail. Running english spins the cue ball in the direction that causes it to widen the angle between (a) the path of the cue ball to the rail and (b) the path that the cue ball takes after it leaves the rail. The opposite of running english is called "reverse" english. (Some players call this hold-up english.)

Illustration 12 shows examples of both running and reverse english. The black line in this illustration

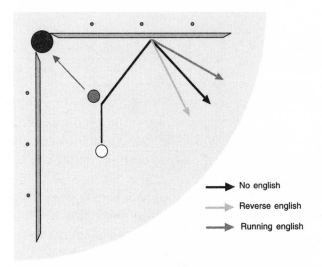

➤ No english

➤ Reverse english

➤ Running english

ILLUSTRATION 12

shows the path of the cue ball when it's stroked with center ball. When running english is applied (right-hand english in this example), the cue ball leaves the cushion spinning in the same direction in which the ball is heading and thus creates a wider angle, as shown by the dark gray line in illustration 12. With reverse english (left-hand english in this example), the angle at which the cue ball leaves the rail narrows, as shown by the light gray line.

Throw—Deliberate and the Other Kind

Now that you've seen how english works on the cue ball, let's look at its effect on the object ball. Put simply, english reverses itself between balls. When a cue ball with right english contacts an object ball, left english is applied to the object ball and the object ball curves to the left. This curving effect is sometimes called throw. Left english on the cue ball will apply right english to the object ball, and the object ball will be thrown to the right. An easy way to remember this is to think of the gears of a machine. When one gear is spinning in one direction, it causes the gear next to it to spin in the opposite direction.

See illustration 13. Here, left english is being applied to the cue ball. The rotation of the cue ball is shown by the arrows surrounding it. When the cue ball contacts the object ball in the illustration, the rotation on the cue ball (left english) causes the object ball to rotate in the opposite direction (right english), just like a set of gears.

Sometimes, even when the cue ball is struck with *no* english, the object ball is thrown. This tends to happen most frequently on thinner cut shots, and it has an effect

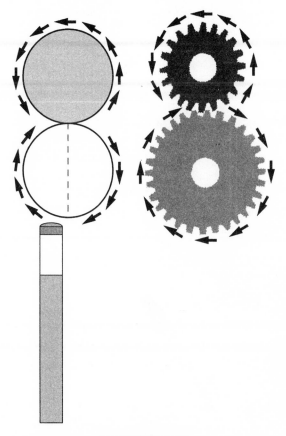

ILLUSTRATION 13
English reverses between balls. Thus, after left english is applied to the cue ball, the cue ball will apply right english to the object ball at the moment of contact. (In other words, the object ball will spin in the direction opposite that which the cue ball is spinning in.) The way that english reacts between the balls is similar to the way that gears in a machine spin.

similar to undercutting the shot. Take another look at illustration 11. Let's assume that you're stroking the cue ball exactly along the centerline. Even though you aren't applying any english to the cue ball, the cue ball will be brushing against the right edge of the object ball. This will cause the object ball to spin somewhat as it heads toward the pocket, as if the object ball had been struck to the right of its centerline. In other words, slight right english is applied to the object ball inadvertently and, if you are not careful, the object ball will miss to the right of the pocket—just as if you had undercut the shot.

To counteract this effect on those shots where it shows up, you must either cut the ball slightly more or add a touch of outside english. Thus, if you are cutting the object ball to the left, as in illustration 11, you must apply right english to the cue ball; if you are cutting the object ball to the right, apply left english. Practice and observation will teach you when this adjustment must be made. Once you're aware of this effect you can make the necessary adjustment, which can become second nature—in essence, a part of how you see or visualize certain types of shots.

On *all* shots struck with english, *speed is critical.* Maximum english is achieved with minimum speed. Since the amount of curve effect is directly related to the amount of friction or traction between the ball and the cloth of the table, a softer stroke allows the object ball to grab the cloth more—which allows the object ball to curve more. When players talk about hitting a shot with english softly to allow the english to "take," this is what they are describing.

Hitting the cue ball slightly to the left or right of center can throw a shot off line (intentionally or accidentally) by a great margin. Over the length of a 9-foot pool table, hitting the cue ball off center by the width of one cue tip might cause the object ball to throw a full diamond or more to the right or left. Then again, it might not . . . and that's the problem.

Many factors affect how much the object ball is thrown. They include:

- **How far off the centerline the cue ball is struck.** The farther from the center line, the greater the spin on the cue ball—but also, the greater the squirt effect.
- **The speed of the shot.** The slower the shot, the greater the effect of the english.
- **Whether the cue ball is being struck with draw.** Stroking the cue ball with draw while applying english accentuates the english.
- **The distance the cue ball travels until it reaches the object ball.** The longer the distance, the more the cue ball curves before reaching the object ball—but the less the object ball is thrown.
- **The distance the object ball travels until it reaches the pocket.** The longer the distance between the object ball and the pocket, the more the object ball can be thrown.
- **The type of cloth on the table.** The cloth content, the type of weave, whether the cloth has a nap, and the direction of the nap all affect how much the english will take.
- **The humidity in the room.** On a rainy or muggy day in a room with no air-conditioning, the throw effect is exaggerated.
- **Whether the cue ball and object balls are clean.** If the balls are dirty, they will act unpredictably, sometimes curving a lot and sometimes not at all.

The list goes on. Any factor that impacts friction will affect how far off line a shot will throw or move. When you are in dead stroke, that elusive zone where everything goes right, you may be able to perfectly adjust for all of these factors. Most times you will not. For that reason, when there is a lot riding on a critical shot in a critical game, the best players will make absolutely sure that they pocket the ball (or *cinch* the shot) by applying no intentional english whatsoever. They may also hit the shot a little more firmly, which reduces any effect from unintentional english and also minimizes the effect of any unevenness in the roll of the cloth or table bed.

Accounting for Speed and Distance

English makes it possible for you to pocket certain shots—if you play them at the proper speed—that appear impossible. Players frequently pass up shots based on a belief that an obstructing ball is too much in the way to allow the cue ball to contact the object ball at the proper point. Many of these shots, however, can be thrown, or curved, into the pocket *without* a massé stroke (that is, without extreme elevation of your rear hand). One of the keys to making these shots is to stroke the cue ball *absolutely as slowly as possible*. The shot must be stroked so softly that the object ball just barely reaches the pocket and drops when it finally gets there (that is, the object ball does not even have enough pace to reach the back of the pocket).

Illustration 14 provides an example. In this illustration I would like to pocket ball A, but ball B appears to be in the way. There is no way I can make ball A in the corner pocket using center ball. The solution is to apply extreme right-hand english and stroke the cue ball with the slowest speed possible. If you practice this shot and become comfortable with it, you'll soon be able to pocket many shots that you previously thought were unmakable.

There are times, however, when a shot should be stroked with a faster-than-moderate speed. For exam-

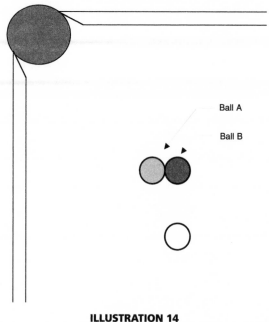

ILLUSTRATION 14

ple, for position purposes you may need to play a nearly straight shot with outside english in order to throw (rather than cut) the object ball into the pocket. This type of shot is easier to make with greater consistency if you stroke firmly. Hitting softly only makes matters more difficult because, at slower speeds, small differences in the speed of the stroke will greatly affect how much the object ball throws. Hit these shots with a firmer stroke and you will still make them—even if your speed is slightly greater or less than you'd planned on.

This variability is why excessive and unnecessary english must be avoided. If you make a center-ball stroke on the cue ball and the speed of your stroke is a little less or more than you anticipated, you will still make the shot. If you try the same shot with english and your speed is slightly off, you may miss the shot altogether because the object ball threw either too much or not enough.

An important factor to consider when applying english is the distance between the object ball and the pocket. If your objective is to make a shot by throwing (rather than cutting) the object ball in, the shot becomes much easier if the object ball isn't too close to the pocket. As the distance between the object ball and the pocket increases, the object ball can be thrown farther. On the other hand, if you need to throw the object ball more than an inch or so, and it's close to the pocket, you will have much more difficulty with the shot.

Uses for English

Having said that english should be minimized by everyone (even skilled players), I must also tell you that to be a top-level player, you must master its use. This is seemingly a contradiction. It is also true. There are certain shots in certain situations, as well as many position options, that you simply cannot execute without english.

When it comes to using english, there is no substitute for practice. Practice applying english at varying speeds and with different variations in the distance between the object ball and the cue ball. Practice shots where the cue ball goes into a rail after pocketing the object ball, but experiment with both running english and reverse english. This is the only way that you will be able to understand how the cue ball and the object ball react—and to apply this knowledge. Practice all shots with both inside and outside english. As in everything else, practice hardest on those shots that make you most uncomfortable.

To speed up your learning process, I've diagramed some shots for which english may be necessary or useful. In illustration 15, ball A is my key ball and ball B is my break ball. The problem is that my shot on ball A is somewhat angled, which will cause the cue ball to move toward the center of the table if I execute the shot with center ball. If that happens, I won't have the angle I need to break into the next frame. See illustration 16. For this reason, the cue ball must be stroked with right english so that ball A can be hit full in the face (or very close to a full-ball hit) yet move to the left and into the upper corner pocket. When executed properly, the cue ball can be made to stop at or near ball A's original position. See illustration 17.

Illustration 18 shows a common break shot. If I stroke this shot with center ball or right english, the likelihood is that the cue ball will end up below the rack at the foot of the table. From that position (zone A in illustration 19), I am not likely to end up with a suitable shot to continue my run. This break shot must instead be stroked with high reverse english—in this case, left english. Such left english will cause the cue ball to run off three rails to end up near the center of the table, where many more shot opportunities will be available. See illustration 20. Many players know how this shot should be played, but far fewer can execute it with the proper english and speed. With a little practice, you will become confident with this shot. Since the object ball is fairly close to the corner pocket, your aim need not be absolutely perfect. Visualize the proper aiming point, take your usual number of practice strokes, and concen-

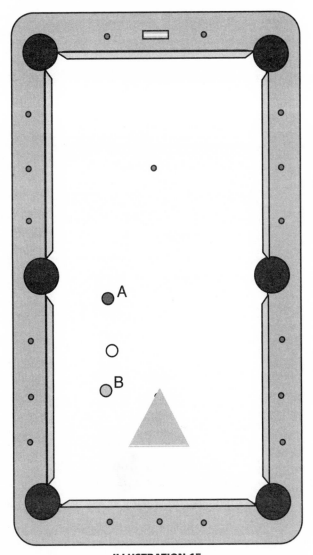

ILLUSTRATION 15
Here, I've ended up with more angle on ball A (my key ball) than I'd like.

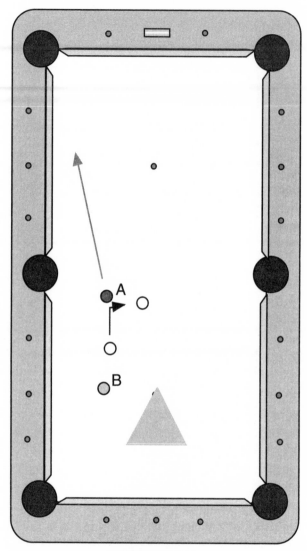

ILLUSTRATION 16

As a result, the natural path of the cue ball will take it toward the center of the table when stroked without english, leaving me too straight for a break shot off ball B.

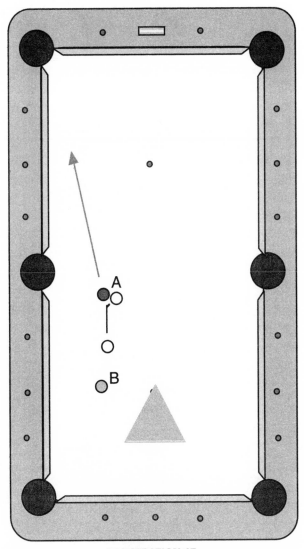

ILLUSTRATION 17
Right english allows me to pocket ball A with a full hit. The cue ball moves much less, and I am able to maintain an angle on ball B for a break shot.

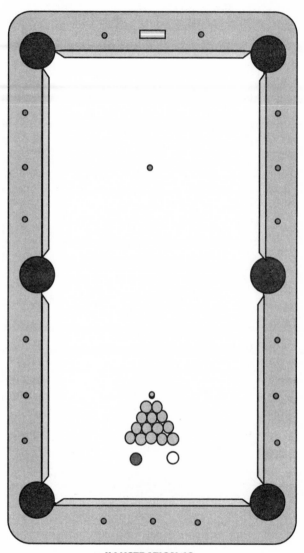

ILLUSTRATION 18

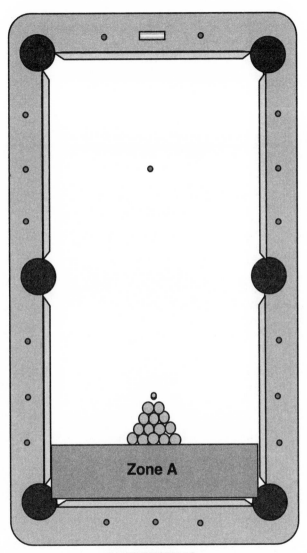

ILLUSTRATION 19

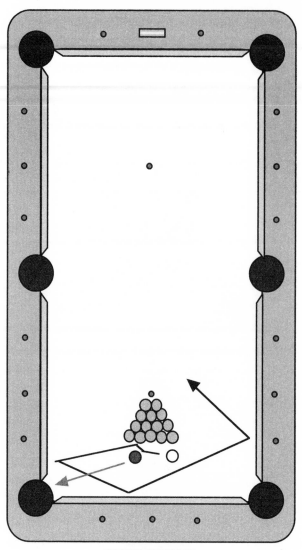

ILLUSTRATION 20

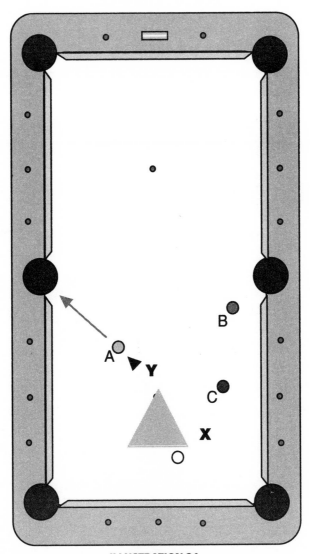

ILLUSTRATION 21

If I had ended up at point X, as I had planned, I could play ball A in the side pocket with slight draw to get to point Y, and then simply stop the cue ball off a shot on ball B (my key ball) in the opposite side pocket. I would then be in perfect position for my break ball (ball C).

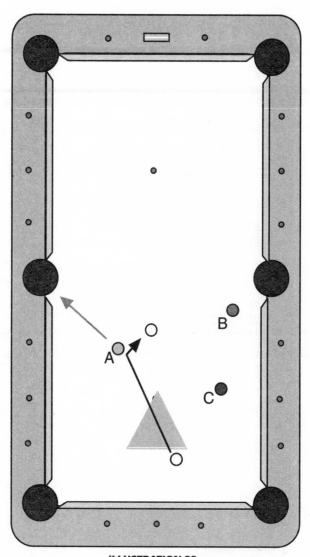

ILLUSTRATION 22

Rather than sending the cue ball loose for position off one or more rails, I choose to control the cue ball and leave myself a deliberately thin cut on the key ball (ball B). This thin cut will allow the cue ball to travel nearly straight into the rail, as shown in the next illustration.

trate on the english you will be applying to the cue ball and the speed of your delivery.

Illustration 21 shows a layout after I missed my intended position. I meant to end up at point X. From there I could have pocketed ball A with slight draw, ended up at point Y, and then simply stopped on my key ball, ball B, in order to end up with an ideal break shot on ball C. Instead, I've created the layout shown in illustration 21. How can I get back in line so that I can break into the next rack?

Instead of trying to send the cue ball up and down the table to end up with an acceptable shot on the key ball, I would choose instead to leave myself with a thin cut on my key ball. See illustration 22. I know that the thin cut on ball B into the side will allow the cue ball to travel (more or less) straight to the rail. With such a thin cut on the key ball, I can stroke the cue ball with extreme left english and then spin it off the rail for a satisfactory break shot. The end result is shown in illustration 23.

Avoiding english is usually the goal. When it must be used, however, your ability (honed through practice) to do so—including the making of shots that require extreme english—will get you out of jams, as shown by the above example.

It's also a good idea simply to practice hitting an object ball straight ahead, but with english. This will help you develop a feel for how far you will be able to throw a shot if you need to. Try shots of all different lengths and at different speeds. Try pocketing a straight-in shot with varying amounts of both left and right english to develop awareness of how much you will need to adjust your point of aim.

When the *appropriate* time comes up in a game to apply english—and not before—you will be ready.

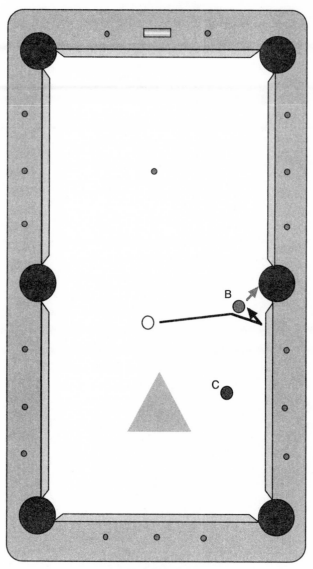

ILLUSTRATION 23

CHAPTER

Minimizing Cue Ball Movement

I absolutely loved to watch Ralph Greenleaf play pool. When I was a teenager, if I heard that Greenleaf was playing a tournament or exhibition anywhere that was humanly possible for me to travel to, I'd find a way to get there. I watched him so much, and studied how he planned his frames so closely, that I could call his shots in my head (before Greenleaf actually played them) and get two racks in a row right.

Greenleaf hardly moved his cue ball. He was the master at minimizing cue ball movement. How skillful was Greenleaf at controlling the cue ball? I once saw him run 60 balls and only hit the rail with the cue ball two times over the whole run!

Perhaps the most common complaint you'll hear from pool players is their own lack of consistency. Everyone's game varies from day to day, but for some reason, some players are steadier than others. Even on their bad days, they can put together decent runs. It almost seems as if the game is always easier for them.

It is. The consistent player has learned the importance of minimizing cue ball movement. When the cue ball travels the shortest distance possible, less can go wrong. Even if a consistent player is having a tough time controlling cue ball speed on a particular day, it won't be as noticeable, since he or she will still retain more control over the table. On the other end of the spectrum are players who can pocket balls but also play position such that the cue ball is constantly traveling. When things are going right for these players, their games inspire awe (especially in the eyes of less knowledgeable observers). On good days these players can make the cue ball hit two or three cushions on every shot and stop like magic at precisely the right spot. On bad days they can't run five balls.

Assuming that I've convinced you that less is more when it comes to cue ball movement, how is it done? First, play for stop-ball position whenever you can, stopping the cue ball at the spot it impacts the object ball. Opportunities to build runs based on stop shots arise more often than most players think. Very advanced players will sometimes observe, at a given point in a frame, that they can run the rest of the rack without touching a rail—or without touching another ball, or both! This happens when the balls are not clustered and few of them are near the rails. These advanced players have trained themselves to look for stop-shot opportunities, and they can run a rack without contacting a rail by recognizing a stop-ball pattern and then executing a series of successful stop (or controlled draw or follow) shots.

This shows why it is important to be able to *execute* a stop shot every time the opportunity arises. Many beginners have difficulty drawing or following the cue ball. More advanced players sometimes have a different problem—they can draw and they can follow, but they have difficulty stopping the cue ball dead in its tracks. Instead, it either lurches forward (accidental follow) or retreats (accidental draw).

The secret to a consistent stop shot is in your rear hand. To stop the cue ball, you must stroke through it—as you must for any shot—but then, after your follow-through, *immediately* and *sharply* stop your rear hand. Failing to stop your rear hand in this manner causes the cue ball to lurch forward when you want it to stop.

The cue ball may also lurch forward due to insufficient speed on the stroke. If you hit too softly, the cue ball picks up forward rotation due to the friction between it and the cloth. Practice stop shots using a striped ball as the cue ball to help gain understanding of the proper speed for a stop stroke.[1] On shorter shots the cue ball *does not roll* on a stop shot; it merely slides—as if on ice—with no forward rotation. You can see this effect on a striped ball if you position the stripe across the equator. (Stopping the cue ball on longer shots is more difficult, but you still need to make sure the cue ball is not rotating forward *at the time the cue ball impacts the object ball.* A moderately forceful draw stroke is required so that, by the time

---

[1]But note that if any chalk is left on object balls, this can cause the balls to react in funny ways in a game. Make sure you wipe clean any object balls you use as practice cue balls.

the cue ball reaches the object ball, it has not picked up any forward rotation.)

A basic nine-ball application exists in ball-in-hand situations. In illustration 24 I have ball in hand on the seven-ball and want an angle on the eight-ball so that I can move the cue ball to get position on the nine-ball. Two easy side-pocket shots are available to me. Since I have ball in hand, I can shoot the seven in either pocket Y or pocket N. Which would you choose?

To some players, there isn't much of an issue. They'll shoot from whatever side of the table they happen to be closest to, since they are confident they can get an angle on the eight-ball by playing the seven into either pocket. And 99 out of 100 times, they will be correct: Their pocket selection won't matter, since they will pocket the seven and get an angle playing into either side pocket.

I would choose pocket Y. When I play the seven into pocket Y, all I need to do is stop the cue ball for my angle on the eight. With pocket N, I need to either follow the cue ball an inch or so or draw it an inch or so. While I'm sure I can properly stroke the seven into pocket N with draw or follow 999 times out of 1,000, I can stop the cue ball by playing the seven into pocket Y 1,000 out of 1,000 times. For this reason, I'll choose the stop-ball option into pocket Y every time, and avoid what amounts to a very small risk . . . even if I need to walk to the other side of the table.

Here's a straight pool example. Look at illustration 25. Ball C is the obvious key ball, allowing the next rack to be broken off break ball D. It's tempting to try to end the rack with an easy shot into side pocket X. This can be done by playing ball B first, then following the cue ball off the head rail (or drawing it back and across the table) for position on A into corner pocket W. Then all

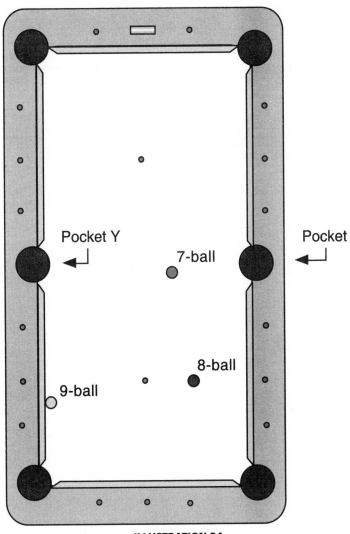

ILLUSTRATION 24

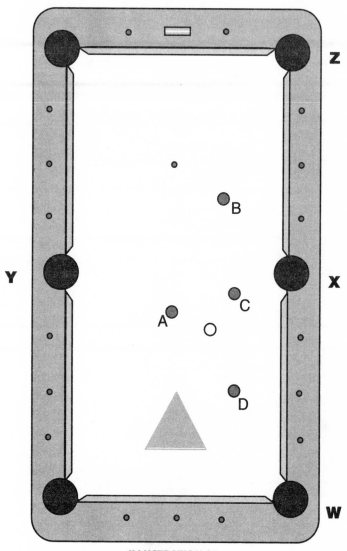

ILLUSTRATION 25

that's left is an easy stop shot on C into the side. Another way to play ball C into pocket X is to play ball A first, then draw off ball B for position on ball C in the side.

I would pass on both of those patterns. I can assure myself of a break shot by playing a stop–stop–stop pattern to finish off the rack. Ball A goes into pocket Y. Stop the cue ball. Then play ball B into pocket Z, again stopping the cue ball. Then all that's left is an easy stop shot, but ball C goes into pocket W.

It's great when you have the chance to run balls using only stop-ball position. My point, however, involves more than merely looking for stop-shot opportunities. The point is to *minimize* cue ball movement. When you must move the cue ball, plan for the shortest available route.

When a stop-ball sequence is not possible, be sure to maintain an angle on each shot. As most players are aware, unlike straight-in shots—which limit you to stop, straight draw, and straight follow—angled shots allow you to move the cue ball from one shot to the next.

The farther you need the cue ball to travel, the greater the angle you'll need on your shot. When you need to move the cue ball only slightly, however, a slight angle is all that's necessary.

Exactly how much of an angle you will need on your shots depends on the speed of the table. If it's very slow, you will need to play position to create more of an angle than you might otherwise choose. By doing so, you will be able to move the cue ball from shot to shot without hitting it too hard. (Every time you hit a shot hard, you reduce the chance that the pocket will accept the ball. At faster speeds, the object balls do not fall into the pocket unless the shot is hit cleanly—without touching a rail or either side of the pocket. Stroking shots at a slow to moderate speed thus makes the pockets bigger.

Your aim may be slightly off in either direction, or you may *need* to favor one side of a pocket over the other to play position or to avoid another ball, but the pocket will accept the ball anyway.)

When a table plays extra fast, you will need to play for less of an angle on your shots. You may also try to use more rails for position. Rails take speed away from the cue ball. When a table plays fast, most of the position errors occur in the field of the table, away from the rails. If you're on an extra-fast table and find yourself with two position options—one that does not involve a rail, the other option requiring the cue ball to bounce off a rail to the desired spot—take the one-rail option. Similarly, if you have a choice between a one-rail and a two-rail position, you might choose the two-rail option on a fast table, even if you normally would not do so.

Until you have adjusted to the speed of the table, play longer position. Playing position so that the cue ball is only a short distance from your next shot is wonderful for pocketing the balls easily. The problem is that if your speed is even slightly off, you may not have a shot at all. Until you have completely achieved a feel for the speed of a table, don't be too ambitious about getting the cue ball close to the object ball for your next shot. Leave yourself more margin for error; make sure you get *some* type of reasonably makable next shot. As you get used to the table speed, you can play for closer and closer position, and your ease in pocketing balls will increase as your match progresses.

The principle of minimizing cue ball movement should be taken to the farthest degree possible, as seen in illustration 26. In this situation many players will shoot ball A and draw the cue ball for position on ball B because they are more comfortable—due to habit or simply personal preference—drawing the cue ball than following it. Although the draw shot is fairly easy, why move the cue ball 5 inches backward when you get great shape on ball B by moving the cue ball only 1 or 2 inches forward? Less can go wrong. Less will go wrong. (For example, you are less likely to end up too close to ball B for a shot.) Even if using draw could give you shape in this situation 99 times out of 100, you can get position using follow (and moving the cue ball a shorter distance) *every* time—100 times out of 100. Minimize your risk. Even if the risk is tiny, minimize it to the point where success is a certainty. The game is more fun that way.

Understanding this principle is part of what separates players who can run 100s from those who run 50s. It's also what separates players who can run an occasional rack from those who can't. Minimizing cue ball movement applies at every level of ability.

Since minimizing cue ball movement helps generate successful runs, you should generally clear off one section of the table at a time. Provided that you have cleared all clusters and problem balls, and have picked out your break and key balls (see chapter 6, Managing the Frame), you should try to pocket all the balls toward one end of the table before moving to the balls at the other end. In other words, avoid patterns that require you to move the cue ball up and down the table.

Exceptions to the Rule

Are there times when moving the cue ball more, rather than less, is correct? Absolutely, but these exceptions are limited. Let's look at two examples.

Sometimes playing a shorter cue ball route is too risky in terms of cue ball speed. You may need, for example, to cut a shot thinly. In these situations you may

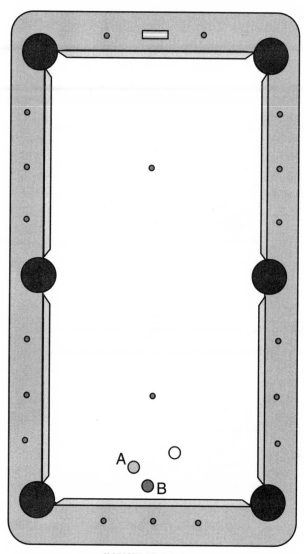

ILLUSTRATION 26

be tempted—for position purposes—to take a shorter route with the cue ball than is sensible. You can see what I mean in illustration 27. I need to cut ball A into one corner and position the cue ball for ball B into the other corner. One approach is to hit the shot softly and try to land at point X, as shown in illustration 28. The drawback of this approach is that, in order to stop at or near point X, I've got to hit the shot so softly that ball A may not have enough speed to reach the pocket. Even if the shot *can* be made (I execute a perfect hit on ball A, at the perfect speed), why accept such a low probability of success when I have a better option?

The better option is to stroke the shot with low running english (in this case, right-hand english) and play the cue ball off three rails, as shown in illustration 29. Although this shot looks fancy, its speed is actually fairly easy to gauge, making this option far superior to trying for the soft hit. Playing the shot this way also allows you to worry less about hitting with perfect speed, which can allow you to focus more on pocketing the ball—further increasing your chances of successfully making the shot *and* obtaining position on ball B.

To the extent that you need to think about speed when playing the three-rail position shown in illustration 29, consider the following: It is far preferable to come up short (that is, to stroke the cue ball too softly) than long (go too far with the cue ball). If you stroke too softly, you will still have some type of shot available on ball B, although it will be farther than you would like. (Just make sure that you stroke the cue ball firmly enough so that you are not blocked by ball C.) On the other hand, stroke too hard and you may scratch in the same pocket into which you shot ball A. Another problem with stroking too hard is that you can end up on or

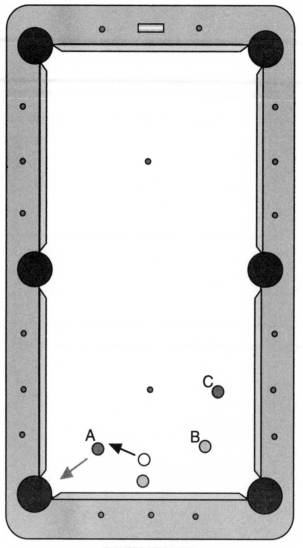

ILLUSTRATION 27

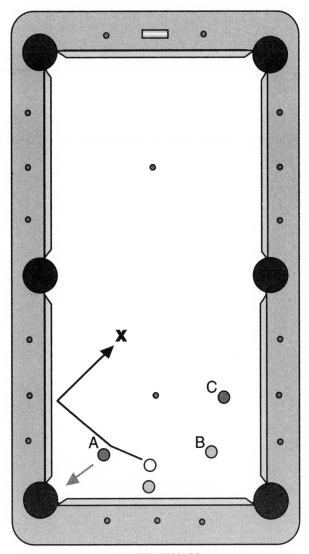

ILLUSTRATION 28

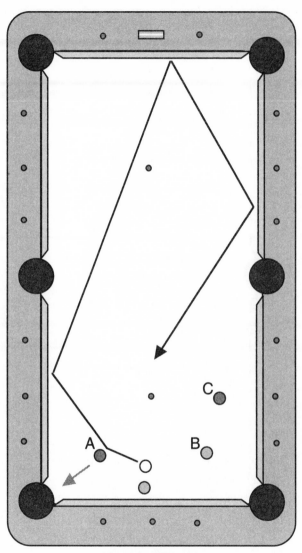

ILLUSTRATION 29

near the foot rail, leaving you without a shot on ball B. For this reason, focus on shooting ball A so that the cue ball has just a bit more speed than it needs to reach the third rail (the right-side rail).

Note: If, in the preceding example, another object ball happened to be available as a back stop for the cue ball, I would take a different approach. Take a look at illustration 30; as you can see, it's exactly like illustration 27, except with additional object balls—most notably ball D—in the lower part of the table. Here, I can run the cue ball into ball D—which will stop the cue ball. Using this technique, I can stroke the cue ball with enough speed to ensure that ball A will have enough pace to reach the pocket. Take care, however, not to stroke this shot excessively hard, since you may drive ball D all the way to the head of the table, where playing position on a shot for this ball may become troublesome. This is one example of playing carom billiards at the same time as playing pool. There are others. (See chapter 6, Managing the Frame.)

Another exception to the rule of minimizing cue ball movement applies when taking a longer cue ball route represents a safer option in terms of getting position for your next shot.

Sometimes a longer route is safer because it allows you to avoid a scratch. Take a look at illustration 31. In this situation many players will play the cue ball with low outside (left) english, drawing it back and forth across the table for two-rail position on ball B, as shown. One significant problem with that approach, however, is the risk of a scratch in side pocket X.

The longer, but safer, route is to stroke the cue ball with high inside (right) english. In this case right english is running english, and allows the cue ball to run three rails for position. Illustration 32 shows the cue ball

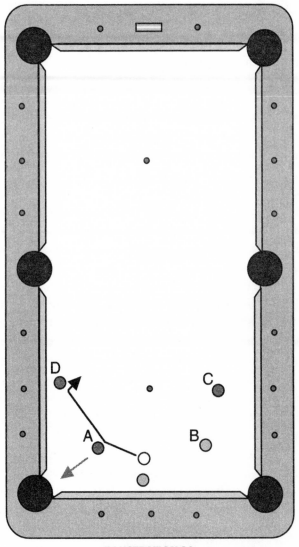

ILLUSTRATION 30

path for this position route. Breaking the general rule of minimizing cue ball movement makes sense in this situation, because it takes the risk of a scratch completely out of the shot.

The three-rail route in illustration 32 gains you another advantage. In chapter 3, Pocketing Balls, I discussed the line between the object ball and the pocket. In this case the line between the object ball and the pocket is shown in gray in illustration 33. (For the purpose of discussing position, I've extended that line through the object ball in this illustration.) When I try the two-rail position shown in illustration 31, my margin for error is slight because the cue ball must travel *across* the extended line connecting ball B and the pocket. If I'm a little too fast or a little too slow, I'll be "out of line"—I won't have a desirable shot.

When I take the three-rail route, however, the cue ball travels roughly *along* the extended line connecting the pocket and the object ball. Again, see illustration 33. My margin for error is now much greater. So long as I stroke the cue ball hard enough to bounce off the third rail—but not *so* hard that I run into the ball I plan to play next (ball B)—I will have an acceptable shot.

Thus, in this last example, there were two good reasons to play longer position. Usually there are none. In general, then, you should minimize your cue ball movement to achieve longer and longer runs. Leave the showy position plays to your opponent. At the same time, keep your mind open and consider all of your position options. The best players move the cue ball the least, and only when necessary.

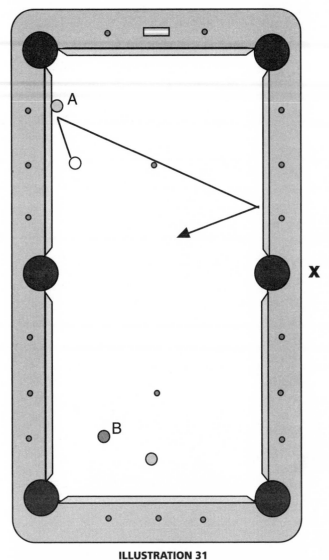

ILLUSTRATION 31
One position option is to draw the cue ball two rails for a shot on the ball B.

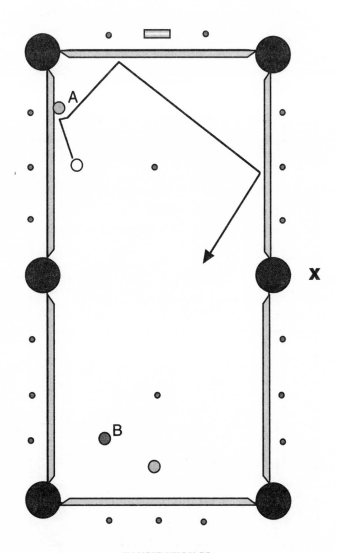

ILLUSTRATION 32
A better possibility is to play three-rail position. Now the risk of a scratch
in side pocket X no longer exists.

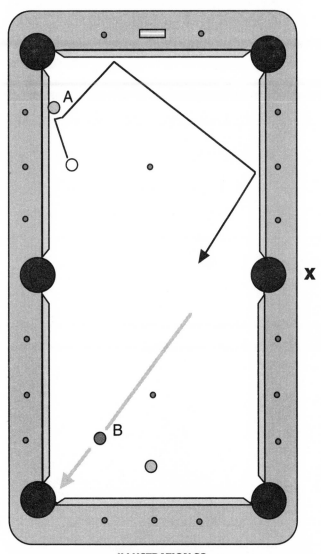

ILLUSTRATION 33

An added bonus to playing the three-rail route is that the cue ball travels on a more natural position path. Unlike the two-rail route, you are no longer crossing the extended line connecting your next object ball and the pocket. Instead, your cue ball is traveling roughly *along* that line, giving you more of a margin for error with your cue ball speed.

CHAPTER

Managing the Frame

Luther Lassiter was one of the most talented players who ever lived. He had to be, given his style of play. After I beat him for the World's Professional title in 1964, he asked me, "Babe, how come you always end up with a break shot?"

I have always said that most players do not go to work soon enough. What I mean is that after their break shot, most players do not determine what their plan of attack will be. *Immediately* after the balls have been broken, you must start to execute a plan to end up with a satisfactory break shot and to eliminate all of the problems in the frame. Your targets are clusters of balls and balls up table that are not hangers—those easily made balls close to the pocket.

If you are lucky enough to end up with a hanger near one of the upper corner pockets, leave it there until you know you will safely clear the rest of the frame. Those "lone rangers" can save you if you encounter trouble in the rest of the rack—for example, if your cue ball ends up frozen to an object ball, or if you miss your position and leave yourself no shot for the intended pocket. Illustration 34 depicts both types of up table balls—problem balls and lone rangers.

Never allow yourself to lapse into pocketing balls simply because they're there—with no plan. Always have some design or goal in mind. Otherwise you are introducing luck into a game where very little luck need be involved. You cannot afford merely to pocket all of the easily makable balls just because you can. Why not? Because in nearly every frame you play, the layout will contain some problems that need fixing. A break ball may not be immediately available, balls may be grouped into a cluster, and the like. Any easy shots—the kind that less experienced players pick off right away—are opportunities.

You must make the best use of the layout's opportunities (the easy shots) to work out ways that solve its problems, by creating break balls or separating clusters. If you squander these opportunities by clearing off your easily makable shots with no plan, you will find that as you get farther and farther into the frame, you'll be stuck with more and more problems—but fewer and fewer ways to correct them.

In terms of shot selection, neglecting this important concept is by far the most common mistake I see. Even some very experienced players make the mistake of not solving problems immediately—although for such play-

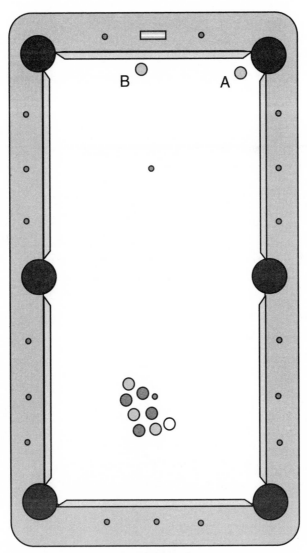

ILLUSTRATION 34

A "lone ranger" (ball A) will save you in situations such as this (unless you've pocketed it too soon in the rack).

Ball B, on the other hand, is a problem ball, which should be cleared as early in the frame as possible.

ers the source of the problem is usually laziness or fear of missing rather than an inability to execute properly. The next question is: How do you go to work early in a frame?

As soon as the rack is broken (whether or not you are the shooter), you should identify its problem areas. Next, think about how you will solve those problems. Is there a problem cluster? If so, what balls are available nearby that will let you separate the cluster? Is there a ball stranded at the head of the table, and what pattern allows you to get position on that ball *as soon as possible?*

A fair amount has been written about "manufacturing" break balls. I agree that you should play billiards while you play pool—pocketing one ball while moving a second object ball to a spot where it becomes a break-ball candidate. There is much more to this concept, however, than merely pushing object balls out from the rack area. This is part of going to work early.

Don't Limit Yourself to One Break Ball

How many runs end because a player fails to get position on a good break ball? The solution to that problem is to give yourself more to choose from. When you get to the end of a frame, then, the additional options will make it much more likely you'll be able to continue your run in some fashion. I am somewhat unusual, even among world-class players, in that I will move balls to create an additional break ball even if I already have one (or two) available to me. Many books tell you not to move object balls (especially not makable ones) unnecessarily. This is a general rule and I agree with it. Manufacturing break balls is an exception, however. And in any event, you should guard against the risks created by moving balls (for the most part, getting "snookered"[2]) by making sure you are playing the simplest position possible for a next shot at the same time that you're manufacturing a break ball, preferably a shot that is guaranteed to be available even if your hit on the prospective break ball is slightly off.

This is no different from the insurance ball concept. An insurance ball is a next shot that you know will be available no matter what. Illustration 35 provides an example. By shooting ball A with center ball and at medium speed, you will open up the cluster of balls above it, giving you a good chance of ending up with a shot on either ball B or one of the balls in the cluster. There is no guarantee, however, that you'll end up with a shot on one of those balls. It is thus critical that you leave ball C on the table until you play ball A. Do not make the mistake of playing ball C first. C is an ideal insurance ball—because when you play ball A, the cue ball is moving away from ball C. For this reason, the clustered balls cannot interfere with a shot on ball C, and you are assured of having that ball available for your next shot.

Be Creative

Don't think only of pushing an object ball out of the rack area. Consider also pushing balls *down* and *up*. Illustrations 36 and 37 give you an idea of what I mean.

---

[2]Getting snookered means ending up without a shot because an object ball obstructs the path between the cue ball and a desired object ball.

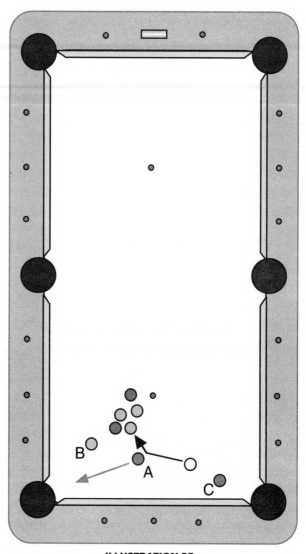

ILLUSTRATION 35

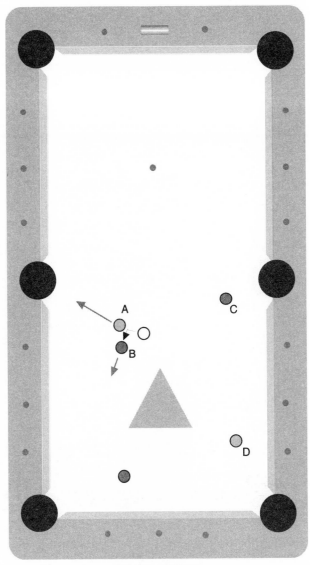

ILLUSTRATION 36

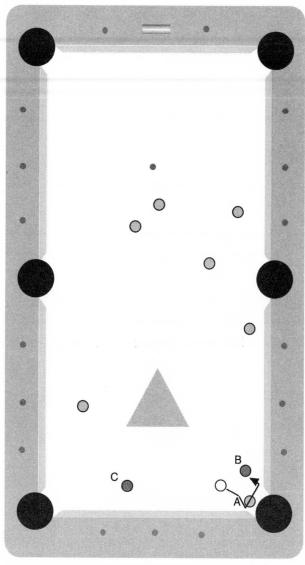

ILLUSTRATION 37

In illustration 36 I am in ideal position to play ball A in the side pocket and, at the same time, nudge ball B down toward the rack area for a break ball. Balls C and D are insurance balls.

In illustration 37 I can play ball A with high left english. My goal is to follow the cue ball so that it rolls into ball B, pushing ball B up for a break ball. Note that as long as I can get a fairly full hit on ball B, I will be guaranteed a shot on ball C—my insurance ball—after pocketing ball A. There are no limits on how you can create, or improve upon, a break ball.

Now look at illustration 38. Here, I will pocket ball W and move ball B in, toward the rack, to create a better break ball. Why? For one thing, this is a very low-risk shot. I *know* that I will end up with a shot on ball X next, which is the next ball I'd like to clear from the table in any case, since it blocks other balls from a clear path to the pocket. If something unexpected happens, balls Y and Z are other next-shot opportunities. Ball A will be my key ball.

Illustration 39 depicts a different situation altogether. I can still move the break ball (ball B) while pocketing ball W, but I won't. Here, I'll draw off ball W to make sure that I *don't* hit ball B. What's different in illustration 39 from illustration 38? Lots. In illustration 39 ball A's location makes it an ideal key ball for ball B as a break ball—*leaving ball B where it already lies.* With ball A as a last shot in the frame, I can easily get the cue ball to rail R. There is no reason to move ball B, so why take any risk at all? What's more, there are fewer balls left in the frame shown in illustration 39 than there were in illustration 38, and there are no insurance balls (that is, there's nothing like balls Y and Z in illustration 38).

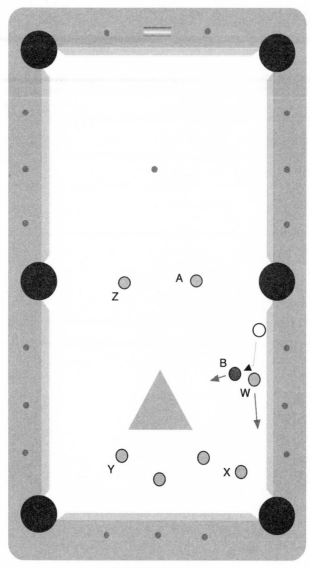

ILLUSTRATION 38

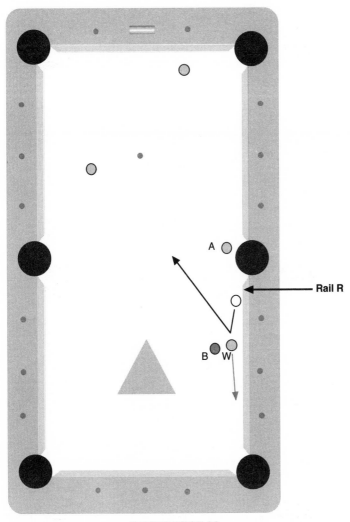

ILLUSTRATION 39

Also, the few balls left in illustration 39 are all up table. Making matters worse, in order to move ball B in illustration 39, I would need to follow the cue ball while pocketing ball W, moving me *farther* from the remaining balls (other than my break ball) and forcing me to take a long shot next, unless I am willing to sacrifice either my break ball or my key ball.

Being creative should not be limited to creating break-ball opportunities. You should also consider pushing *key* balls into position. The best way to assure position on a break ball is to have the luxury of playing for a key ball near a side pocket. A key ball in such a position is worth quite a lot, since it can be pocketed in several pockets, will never be a very long shot, and, in every way, gives you many options at the end of a rack.

Recognize Billiards and Combinations

There is no rule that says only the cue ball can be used to create break balls or to break up clusters. Sometimes an easy billiard or combination will pop up that will produce a break ball or separate a problem cluster.

Let's look at illustration 40. The combination shot (pocketing ball Z off ball Y) is practically unmissable. There is little doubt that if you strike ball Y with the cue ball with at least a minimal amount of care, ball Z will naturally be directed into the pocket. Now take a look at illustration 41. Note that pocketing ball Z barely becomes more difficult if you hit ball Y with the cue ball after first caroming the cue ball off ball A. The benefit of playing the shot in this way is that you can turn ball A into a break ball. Simply nudge ball A directly into the

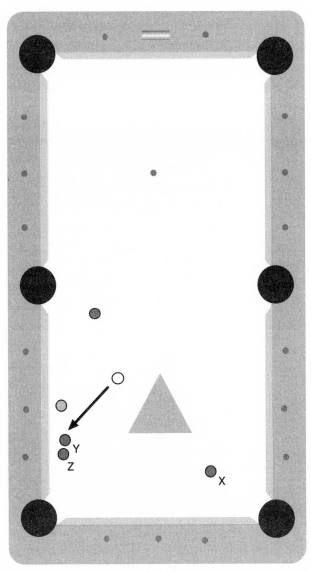

ILLUSTRATION 40

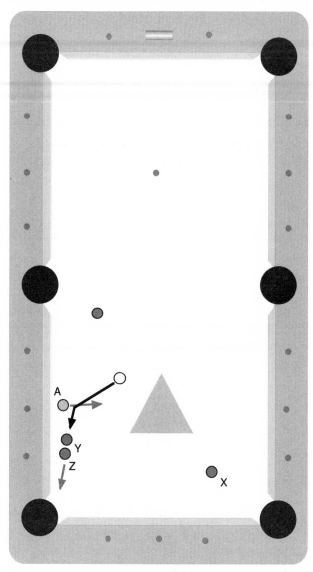

ILLUSTRATION 41

rail; it must, if struck with the correct speed (softly), bounce straight off the side rail into a position perfect for a break shot. This billiard is not a difficult shot, and, in this example, ball X is available as an insurance shot (although you are also likely to end up with a shot on ball Y).

Sometimes you will be faced with tougher decisions. For example, you may be in a position to play a somewhat riskier shot (such as a combination or a shot that's not perfectly in line) that will allow you to clear a problem ball. Illustration 42 gives you an idea of the type of dilemma I'm talking about. Here, you can play the combination shot now so that ball X will separate the cluster, or choose instead to pass up the combination and attack the cluster later.

Do you take the riskier shot now and try to eliminate the problem immediately, or do you play position on a few more balls so that you can attack the cluster from a different angle?

Your decision should be based on several factors. How far are you into the frame? If you pass up a combination that will clear a problem ball now, will there be enough other balls on the table to bail you out if you fail to execute your pattern perfectly? This is one of the most important factors. You should also scrutinize the opportunity you have now to clear up a problem. How valuable an opportunity is it? If your present opportunity is a combination shot or billiard, is there a chance that the first object ball you strike will interfere with other shots or block the cue ball on your very next shot? If so, there is usually a better pattern available to you. Don't go out of your way to solve one problem when it's likely to create another. (This sounds like simple advice, but the patience and discipline required to pass up a

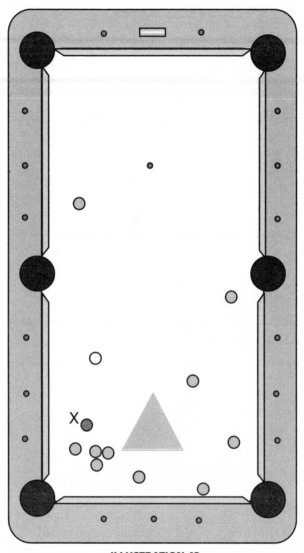

ILLUSTRATION 42

shot are among the qualities that separate top players from all the others.)

There are other questions you must ask yourself. Even if your present opportunity to solve a problem is not ideal, is it realistic that you will get a significantly better opportunity later in the frame? Will waiting to solve the problem provide you a high-percentage opportunity to end up with a better shot at solving the problem later? If the answer to these questions is no, then take your opportunity now—while it's there. Give yourself the best choice—that is, the best choice that is realistically available—to continue your run.

The right choice for you might be the wrong one for someone else. Part of figuring out when to try to solve a problem is being honest with yourself about your own abilities . . . your strengths and weaknesses.

Let me tell you something that may take some pressure off you in terms of position play. Despite what a lot of other professionals may tell you, I believe that there is not always only one correct way to play a frame. No doubt, certain situations may come up that offer a clearly superior choice. But if the choices you made allowed you to get through the frame, they were correct enough. Move on. Don't allow yourself to be paralyzed because a supposedly better player is your opponent or is watching your game. You need not worry about what some other player would do if faced with the same layout. You are the one at the table and the others are sitting down, and that is for a reason. Your opponent either just missed or he or she could not continue a run and was forced to play safe. You don't need to meet anyone's expectations but your own (which should be high, but within reach). Focus on the task at hand.

Shot Selection

What separates experienced 14.1 continuous players from novices is shot selection. Even professionals miss shots from time to time—but the pros generally choose patterns consisting of a series of simple shots that ends with a break shot. Players with lesser shot selection find themselves faced with tougher shots to execute, so their shot-making ability is constantly being tested. Worse still, poor shot selection will eventually end your run: You'll be left without a makable shot or without a break shot at the end of a frame.

One of the most intimidating situations for many players is an open rack with no problem clusters. There are many shots to choose from and no road map for guidance. Unlike nine-ball, you cannot simply play your shots in number sequence. You feel that any shot you take could be a mistake. What do you do?

Go to Work Right Away . . . Again

Although you've cleaned out the most obvious problems, such as clusters, recognize that certain balls (I'll call them secondary problem balls) can still create trouble. Select a pattern that will allow you to pick off these secondary problems right away. Nearly all balls on the rail are secondary problem balls. Generally, these can only be made in two out of the six pockets. And if a rail ball is near a side pocket such that a scratch into the side pocket becomes a risk, for all practical purposes this ball could be makable in only one pocket.

In illustration 43 ball B can pose just this problem. It will be difficult to pocket it into pocket Y without

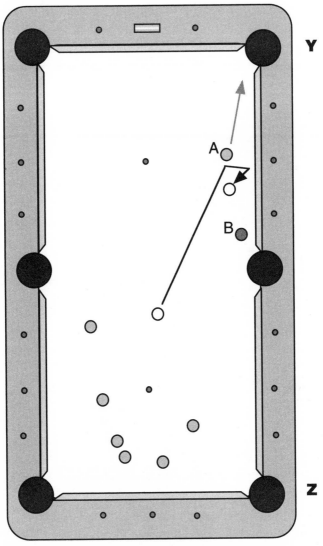

ILLUSTRATION 43

scratching into the right side pocket unless you can control the position of the cue ball so perfectly that it ends
up below the right side pocket and either (a) against the
right side rail or (b) aligned to give you a straight-in
shot into pocket Y. Attack that problem right away. A
good solution would be to play ball A first (although it is
a slightly longer shot than some of your other choices).
This will allow you to get to ball B right away. What's
more, you will be playing ball B into pocket Z, eliminat-
ing any risk of a scratch.

Going to work early also means clearing balls that are
makable but still secondary problem balls, because they
block the path of other object balls to the pocket. If your
cue ball is in a position where you can choose from among
several fairly easy shots, pick the shot that will open up another pocket for an object ball. Do this even if it means
taking a slightly more difficult shot: Lacking the courage
to do this is more likely to end your run than missing the
correct shot would be. No matter what your level of play,
observing this simple rule can extend your runs.

Balls that are makable but very close together are
another type of secondary problem ball. If balls can be
made, try to position your cue ball so you can pocket
those balls rather than taking the risk of disturbing
them and converting makable shots into a problem cluster. The only time it makes sense to run into balls that
are makable as they lie is when doing so will give you
some kind of bonus, such as a break ball. Even then, run
into makable balls only when you are guaranteed a shot
afterward.

Which is not to say that makable balls close together
are not troublesome—they are. Often such balls can be
made in only one pocket, and you'll have to play precise
position on these shots to keep neighboring balls from

getting in the way. As with all problems, address these early. Find a way to get to that precise position sooner rather than later.

In illustration 44, for instance, the two object balls near the left side pocket can each be pocketed as they lie—so don't take the risk of creating a worse situation by running into them. Since they can be pocketed comfortably only from the shaded areas, however, get position on them now by playing ball A right away.

If you go to work early, very few racks are impossible to clear. With practice, you will increasingly find yourself at the point in a frame where you have left yourself both a break ball and a set of remaining object balls that don't interfere with each other and are off the rails.

Finishing Off the Rack

You've done all of the above. You're down to five or six balls in the frame with no two of them touching and you have at least one good break ball along with a key ball.

To finish off the rack successfully, work backward from the key ball. Try to figure out the best route toward falling into position for the key ball. The "best" route means the route involving the least cue ball movement, the least likelihood of the cue ball running into another ball while playing position, and the best chance of making absolutely sure that the cue ball ends up on the correct side of the key ball.

Take a look at illustration 45. Here, it's late in the frame and you have successfully cleared off all problems, leaving six object balls. Ball Z is a perfect break ball. Ball D would be acceptable, too, but ball Z is prefer-

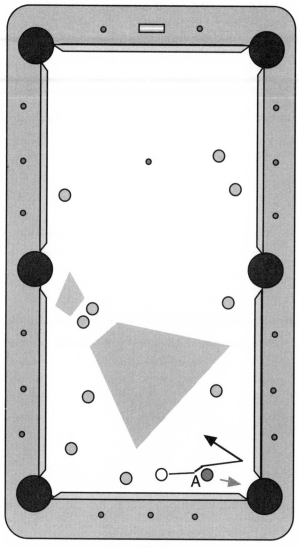

ILLUSTRATION 44

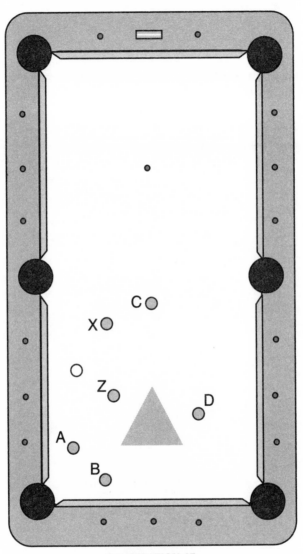

ILLUSTRATION 45

able since ball X is available as an ideal key ball to get to ball Z. How would you proceed?

Work backward. X is your last shot in the frame. Which ball is situated best for position on X? The answer is ball D, which allows you to play ball X in the side and stop for position on ball Z. Ball C lies in excellent shape to get you to ball D; ball B gets you to ball C; and ball A gets you to ball B.

Thus, one simple way to finish this frame is to shoot—in this sequence—A, B, C, D, and, finally, X. As shown in illustration 46, start by drawing off ball A for a shot on ball B into the same pocket. Then draw with running english (hitting the cue ball low and left) to run the cue ball around ball D for a shot at ball C in either side pocket S or corner pocket C. Shoot ball D into the corner pocket. (Given where you ended up in illustration 46, shoot ball D with draw.) Now all that's left is to make ball X, doing your best to leave the cue ball as close to ball X's location as possible. Use a low right hit on the cue ball. After pocketing ball X in the side, you will be left with perfect position on ball Z.

Remember, even at this late stage in the frame, to be flexible. If you miss your position in the final few balls in a frame, make an adjustment and play a different sequence to get on a break ball. You may even need to play a pattern to end up on a different break ball than your first choice. You may also have to change course and end the frame with a safety.

Remaining flexible at all times, based on what has already happened in the frame, is the correct way to play. Do not stubbornly stick to a particular pattern or a particular break ball after the situation has changed. Do not get so angry at yourself for missing position that you find yourself playing patterns you know are too difficult

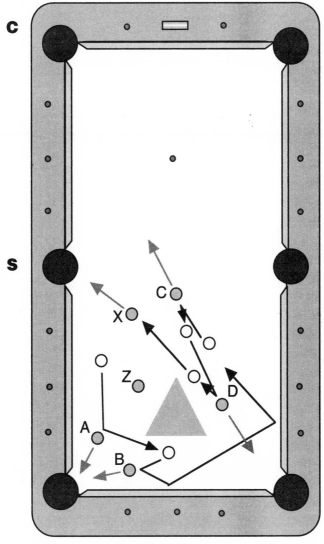

ILLUSTRATION 46

to complete. In those instances it's tempting to go ahead with your original pattern no matter what—so that you can "redeem" yourself by making a fantastic shot, perhaps, or because you wish to aggravate yourself further by digging yourself into a deeper hole. Instead, after every single shot, evaluate anew whether the pattern you originally selected makes the most sense or whether another alternative is now superior. This shot-by-shot reevaluation gives you the best chance at all times to continue your run under the circumstances. Don't get caught up in how easy your run would have been had you only done such and such. Don't get caught up in the past, even the very recent past. Choose your pattern based on what the table presents to you *now*.

When picking an appropriate pattern in straight pool, you must always keep your mind free of those nagging thoughts that so often plague us after we've executed a shot imperfectly. While the game is not as complicated as a lot of people think, it does require your complete concentration. When it comes to pattern play, concentrate on figuring out what is the best pattern realistically available to you given the present layout.

CHAPTER

Break Shots

After seeing all of the billiards champions from the 1920s to today, I feel that Ralph Greenleaf was the best of all time. He had a fluidity that was unmatched, and it showed in his break shots. When Greenleaf hit a break shot, the cue ball often slammed into the rack, retreated due to the force of the impact, and then followed forward to make its way through what was left of the rack a second time.

Straight pool requires a break shot unlike that of any other other billiard game. Only in straight pool does the break shot allow you to run an infinite number of balls in succession. This is part of what makes straight pool exciting at the highest levels. Even if a top player is losing 149 to 0 in a game to 150, he or she might come back in spectacular fashion if allowed only one more inning at the table.

A run of 100 or more balls under match conditions is always exciting—and even for a professional, 100 consecutive balls is a good run. A 100-ball run requires seven successful break shots. Many times, however, a promising run falls apart at the break shot.

This may be because the break shot carries with it more pressure than any other shot in straight pool. Make one and you advance triumphantly into a new frame. Miss one and you turn the game over to your opponent, along with at least one or two easy shots. You'll almost always end up either looking great or looking horrible; rarely will the result be anything between these two extremes.

A Successful Break Shot

You have hit a successful break shot when you:

- Make the called ball.
- Separate balls from the rack.
- Free the cue ball from the rack.

Your objectives should be no less and no more. If you accomplish less than all of these goals, you have probably ended your inning.

But don't try to accomplish more, either. To the extent that there's any luck in this game, it comes into play at this moment. Sometimes you will succeed at achieving all of the above goals and still be left without a shot. Those occasions will be rare. It is true, to some degree, that you can play position off particular types of break shots. For most break shots, however, all this does is add to your worries and increase the chance that you'll miss the shot altogether. Which leads to the next topic.

Keeping Your Nerve

All of the thinking needed to accomplish the critical elements noted above (such as where to aim, what speed to use, whether to follow or draw, whether to apply english) should be done *before* you start your practice strokes. By the time you're getting ready to shoot, the only thought on your mind should be (for example) "I'm going to pocket the ball using left follow at a medium speed." That's it. You don't need to complicate matters by trying to keep track of anything more. If you've thought it out properly beforehand, that's all you'll need.

Selecting Your Break Ball

If you've done a good job managing the frame, you may have several break balls to choose from. Even if your opponent missed late in the frame and you are coming to a table that has only a few object balls left, you have choices—provided you can get the cue ball to the right place—since many types of shots can serve as break balls.

At the same time, several types of break shots are particularly attractive and, for that reason, are commonly played. Almost everyone has his or her favorites. If I have a choice, all other things being equal, I prefer (in this order):

1. A break ball on the right side of the rack (looking at the rack from the head of the table), as shown in illustration 47.
2. A break ball on the left side of the rack.

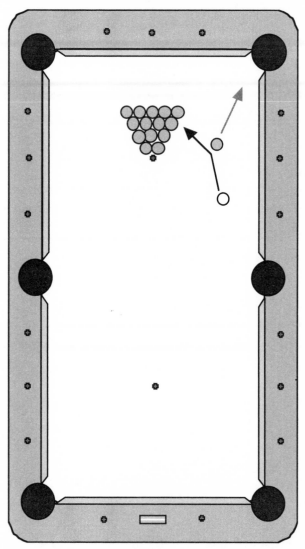

ILLUSTRATION 47

This break shot is ideal, especially for a left-handed player. In general, break shots where the break ball is to the side of the rack, such as this one, are the best. Pocketing the ball is fairly easy, and if the shot is executed properly, you'll be able to free the cue ball.

3. A side-pocket break ball.
4. A break ball behind the rack.

Break balls to either side of the rack are best both because you can break out the object balls toward the corner pockets at the foot of the table, and because it's relatively simple to get the cue ball free and over to the center of the table, from where you're likely to have a shot. A break ball to the right of the rack is better for me than one on the left, since I shoot left-handed and have an easier reach on the right side. Thus, when the break ball is to the right of the rack, I can play position for the cue ball to be closer to the break ball. This increases the likelihood that I'll make the shot *and* be able to control the cue ball. With these two factors going for me, I can apply more pace to the cue ball, which will free more balls from the rack for potential next-shot opportunities. A right-handed player, of course, gains these same advantages with a break ball to the left of the rack.

If I'm playing position for a break ball on the left side of the rack, I must leave the cue ball a little farther away from the break ball. Generally, for break balls to the left of the rack, I need to keep the cue ball near the left side pocket. If it's any closer to the break ball than that, I will need to stretch over too much of the table. If, on the other hand, the cue ball is any farther than that, I've got a long shot. See illustration 48. The opposite is true for you if you are right-handed.

Side-pocket break shots are my next favored break shots; an example is shown in illustration 49. Such break shots tend to do a good job of loosening balls from the rack (that is, they provide good yield). Also, if you draw the cue ball when executing these types of shots, you rarely end up with it frozen to the rack after impact.

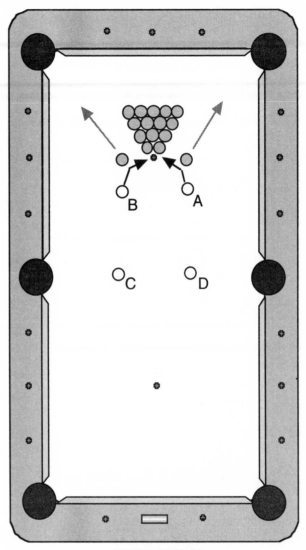

ILLUSTRATION 48

As a left-handed player, I have no trouble leaning over the table for a break shot from position A. On the other side of the table, however, I cannot shoot comfortably from position B, which requires too much of a stretch. When playing position to fall on break balls on the left side of the rack, I strive to position the cue ball farther up the table, about even with the side pockets. Position C is just about perfect for me. The opposite (position D) would apply for a right-handed player.

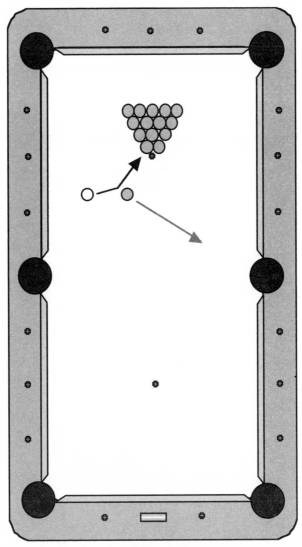

ILLUSTRATION 49

Consider opportunities to break open the rack using side-pocket break shots, such as this one. These shots should be stroked with draw.

Behind-the-rack break shots such as the one shown in illustration 50 also have their advantages, most notably that pocketing the called ball is usually easy. You're shooting into a corner pocket at close range! The drawback is that you need to do something extra to free the cue ball and get it to the center of the table. Otherwise, the cue ball often ends up below the rack of balls, which offers fewer, and less desirable, opportunities for shots after the break. Worse yet, if you're careless, you'll often find yourself *frozen* behind the rack after playing one of these break shots. And even if you're careful, these types of shots carry somewhat more risk of the cue ball running into an interfering object ball (sometimes called a kiss) and ending up in a less-than-ideal position.

Does this mean that if you have a choice you should *always* play for a particular type of break shot (for example, a side-pocket break shot over one behind the rack)? No. You need to weigh several factors.

You may achieve good yield off a particular break ball, but getting position on that break ball may be difficult because of the unavailability of a good key ball. At the same time, you may have another potential break ball that provides you less of a yield but is easy to get to, because getting to the key ball and getting position off the key ball is easier.

Generally, I choose the break ball I *know* I can get instead of trying to play tougher position to get to a "better" break ball (one that offers greater yield). You need to play the percentages, and making dead certain that you'll end up with a break shot (of some sort) is part of that. Also, you need to trust your ability to work with whatever the table gives you to separate clusters after you play the break shot that begins a new frame.

The score will also dictate how you should proceed. In a tight game or at the beginning of a match, I'm less

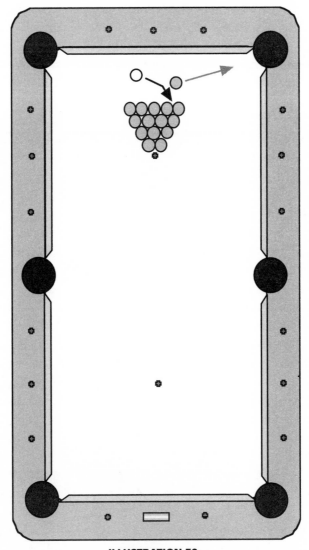

ILLUSTRATION 50
Behind-the-rack break shots have their advantages, but the cue ball can end up stuck toward the foot of the table instead of reaching the table's center, where shots tend to be more available.

concerned with yield; I may take speed off the cue ball to make absolutely certain I will pocket the break ball. If I'm on a run and feel comfortable, I'll pocket the break ball with more speed and move more balls off the rack.

Shooting the Break Shot

It's much easier to explain how to shoot break shots through illustrations than by using words alone. What follow, then, are illustrations of break shots and descriptions of how to approach them. Each break shot that I discuss will be depicted in two illustrations: one showing the layout immediately before the shot, and a second showing the results of a successfully executed break. These results are based on the outcome of actual shots. Like every other aspect of billiards, however, break shots have somewhat different results each time. Thus, the layouts you'll see after you play the various types of break shots shown here will differ from the illustrations, but some general characteristics can be observed.

The fundamental principles to keep in mind all concern getting the cue ball away from the rack after impact. If it hits the rack too slowly, your cue ball may end up frozen to an object ball or too close to an object ball for a shot. The first consideration should be how thin your hit on the break ball will be. If your hit is full (that is, you don't have much of an angle on your shot), much of the energy from the cue ball will be absorbed by the break ball. As a result, after impact with the break ball, the speed of the cue ball will be diminished. For this reason, when confronted with a fuller hit on a break shot, you need to hit with more speed in order to move balls off the rack. In contrast, on a thin hit the cue ball will be traveling with sufficient speed (after contacting the break ball) to move balls off the rack even if you stroke with only moderate speed.

Another consideration is *where* you will be hitting the rack. If the natural path (the tangent line) of the cue ball is toward one of the corners of the rack, you will not need as much cue ball speed, since the cue ball will generally move off the rack nicely with moderate speed. If your cue ball will contact the rack in the middle of one of its sides, however, you must use much more speed, and you'll probably need to draw the cue ball also. Of course, hitting with more speed decreases your chances of pocketing the break ball. So, you see, it is a balancing act.

Break Shots to the Side of the Rack

Illustration 51 depicts an ideal break shot for a right-handed player. The thin cut on the object ball allows you to attack the rack with good cue ball speed using only a medium-speed stroke. This shot should be played with high right english. By playing this shot with a follow stroke, and right english, as suggested, your cue ball should travel to the end rail (rail X) and then back to the center of the table. The results will generally be good, as shown in illustration 52. (If the break ball and cue ball were in corresponding positions to the *right* of the rack, I would address the cue ball with follow and *left* english.)

In illustration 53 the break shot is again to the left of the rack, as it was in illustration 51. The difference is that, in illustration 53, the angle on the break shot is straighter than is ideal. It will be difficult to generate the speed and angle necessary to tear through the corner of the rack, as you were able to do off the break shot in illustration 51. In order to generate the speed

X

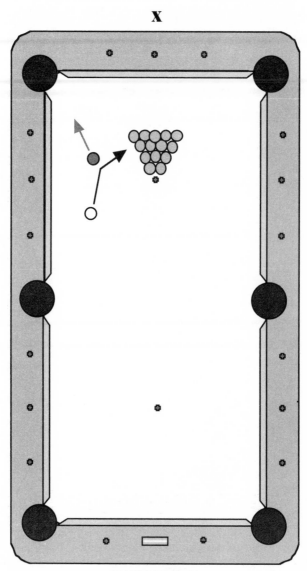

ILLUSTRATION 51
This break shot should be stroked with high right english. The angle and location of the cue ball and break ball are ideal.

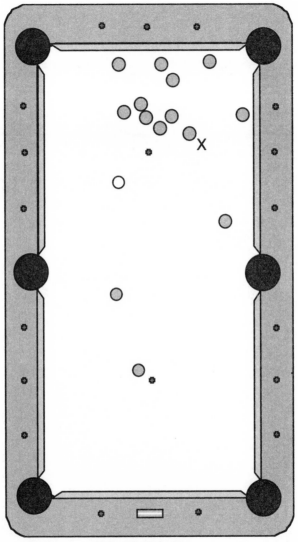

ILLUSTRATION 52

The break shot was a success here, since the cue ball is near the center of the table (from where I'm likely to end up with shots), the balls have spread well, and there is at least one candidate for a break shot into the *next* rack, object ball X.

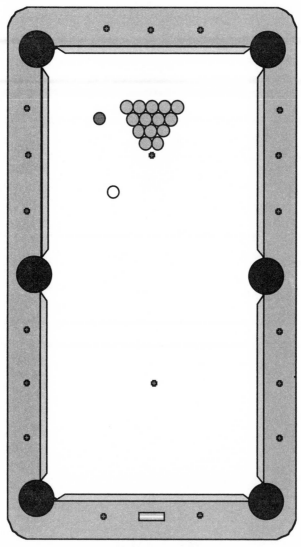

ILLUSTRATION 53
Given how straight the break ball is in this example, and how low it lies in
relation to the rack, trying to force the cue ball through the corner of the
rack is not recommended.

necessary to break the rack in that fashion, you may end up missing the break shot altogether. Also, the break ball is lower on the rack than it was in illustration 51. Here, as shown in illustration 54, you should *follow* the cue ball with high *left-hand* english so that the cue ball can travel two rails (first the foot rail, then the left-hand side rail) to the center of the table, where you will be most likely to end up with a shot on any of the object balls loosened from the rack. The result is shown in illustration 55. Notice that in order to achieve a good spread of the object balls, the cue ball had to be struck forcefully enough to end up toward the head of the table, leaving you with longer shots than the ones shown in illustration 51. The first shot in this frame must now be a longer shot than was necessary from the layout shown in illustration 52.

The break shot shown in illustration 56 is—once again—not at the ideal angle you saw in illustration 51; the angle on this break shot is too straight. Notice also that the cue ball is headed for the middle of one of the rack's sides. This is a problem, because the cue ball will hit the rack of object balls at one of the rack's thickest parts, where it will likely get stuck. With a break shot like the one shown in this illustration, don't try to follow the cue ball through (or off) the rack. The risk of getting the cue ball stuck to the side of the rack (or frozen on an object ball in some other fashion) is too high with that type of approach. Instead, *draw* the cue ball off the rack in order to free the cue ball. Moderate draw is sufficient; you don't want to end up at the head of the table.

Illustration 57 shows the result, which is quite satis-factory. The balls have spread far enough apart to leave you with shots and some opportunities to further break up the rack. Yet the balls did not spread so much that you're left with lots of stray balls toward the head of the

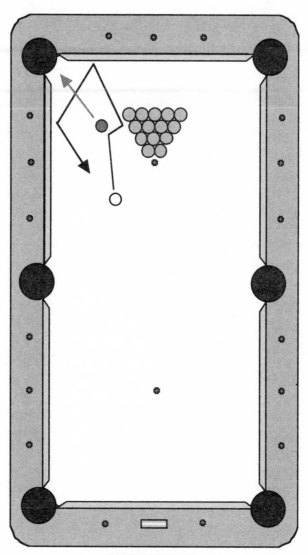

ILLUSTRATION 54

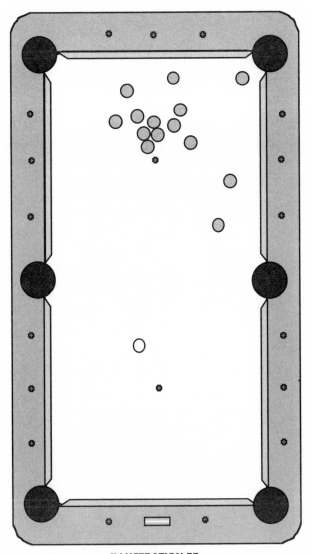

ILLUSTRATION 55

Not a bad result, although the balls have not separated quite as well as shown in illustration 52. In order to spread the object balls *this* much, the cue ball had to be struck fairly hard. As a result, it did not come to rest until it reached the upper part of the table, and thus ended up farther from the object balls than in the prior example.

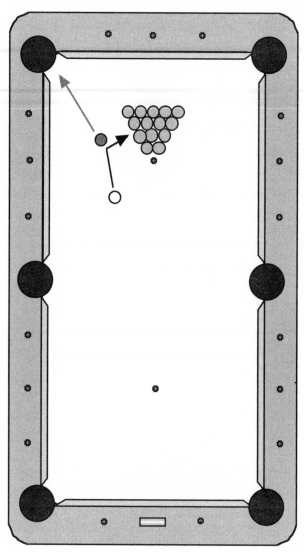

ILLUSTRATION 56

table. This break shot also worked out well in terms of cue ball placement. The cue ball is fairly close to the center of the table, and you're thus in a position to play just about any one of the object balls that have been loosened from the rack.

There are countless types of break shots to the side of a rack. Those I've just described are only some of the more common examples. What these examples teach, however, is how to consider:

- The angle of the hit on the break ball—and thus the natural speed of the cue ball.
- What part of the rack will be struck by the cue ball.
- The angle at which the cue ball goes into the rack.

Keeping these factors in mind will tell you whether the cue ball should be addressed with follow, draw, or center, and left-hand or right-hand english.

Break Shots Above the Rack (Side-Pocket Break Shots)

On side-pocket break shots, such as the one shown in illustration 58, hitting the cue ball with draw will free it after it hits the rack. A draw stroke will also help you avoid a scratch in the near corner pocket (pocket X in the illustration), which will occur with frequency if you strike this break shot with center or high ball (follow). As you can see from illustration 59, the cue ball ended up in the lower part of the table, and the object balls have spread apart well. Only one cluster (marked A in the illustration) might need to be separated, and you can pocket those two balls as they lie (in one of the upper corner

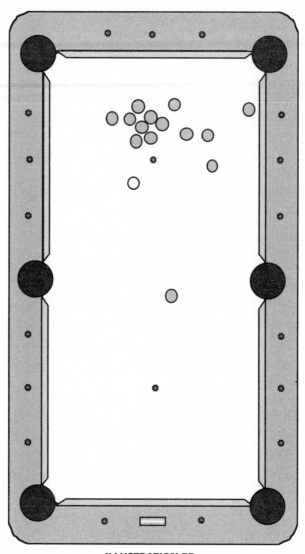

ILLUSTRATION 57
This break shot turned out quite well.

X

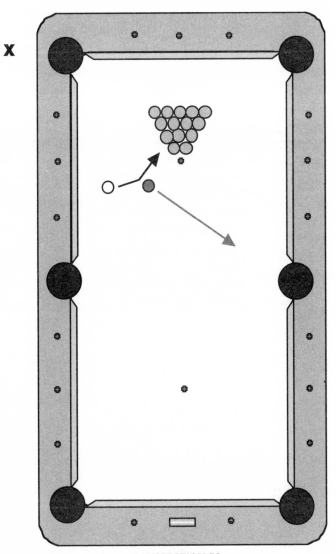

ILLUSTRATION 58

pockets) once obstructing balls B and C are cleared away. (You were somewhat unfortunate with the results in illustration 59 in that the first shot you'll be shooting in this frame is not an easy one.) This break shot should be the subject of one of your practice sessions, since it's often available—yet many players are not accustomed to playing angled shots into the side pockets.

With all break shots, if you can see from the tangent line that your cue ball will be hitting one of the racked balls squarely on the nose, you won't need very much draw to get the cue ball to come off the rack because it will be bouncing off solidly. If instead you will be hitting the rack *between* two balls, the cue ball won't naturally come off the rack as much. You'll need more draw and/or more speed to free the cue ball.

Break Shots Below the Rack

As I've discussed, when it comes to break shots to the side of the rack, whether you stroke the shot with follow or draw, or left-hand or right-hand english, depends on the placement of the break and cue balls. The same is true with break shots below the rack.

In illustration 60 the cue ball is closer to the foot rail than it is to the break ball, which is near a corner of the rack. As in the ideal beside-the-rack break shot (illustration 51), you can use follow to tear through the rack. Here, you should apply follow and right english. The cue ball will follow through the corner of the rack, contact the side rail, and spin toward the right—toward the center of the table. This is one of the easiest break shots to execute. The results are usually very good, as shown in illustration 61. The object balls have spread apart well and the cue ball is in the clear in the center of the table.

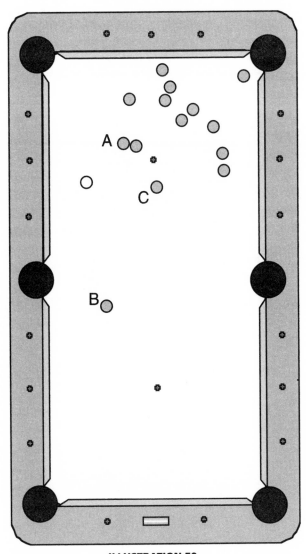

ILLUSTRATION 59

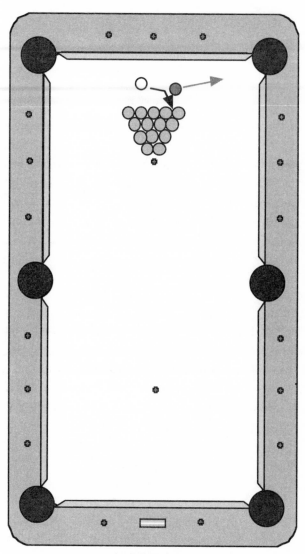

ILLUSTRATION 60

You're not as well off in the next diagram, illustration 62. Here, the object ball and cue ball are positioned at a different angle than they were in illustration 60. The hit on the break shot is more full in illustration 62, so the natural cue ball speed is diminished. It would require an excessively hard stroke to try to tear through the corner of the rack. With the layout shown here, don't try to force the cue ball through the rack with follow. Yes, you will sometimes see players attempt to force the ball through the rack from this position and end up with a shot. Much more often, however, they'll end up stuck without a shot near the foot rail or frozen to an object ball. It's also common for players to miss this shot after trying to force too much speed onto the cue ball in an effort to break through the rack.

The better approach is to stroke the cue ball with high reverse (left) english. The reverse english allows the cue ball to run off three cushions. Your goal is to contact the rack, follow into the side rail, then the foot rail, and, finally, the other side rail and out to the center of the table. See illustration 63. This is a beautiful shot when executed. As with most of the break shots I've discussed in this chapter, when the shot works as planned, the cue ball comes to rest in the center of the table, where you are most likely to have shots available to you.

Still, even if you play this break shot perfectly, you may—as in any other break shot—encounter bad luck in the form of one of the object balls rebounding off a rail then running into the cue ball. A kiss of this type can cause the cue ball to end up in a poor position or even scratch, but you cannot afford to let such possibilities distract you. Remember, you must always focus on correct execution of the shot. Don't worry about kisses and other uncertainties generally beyond your control. This

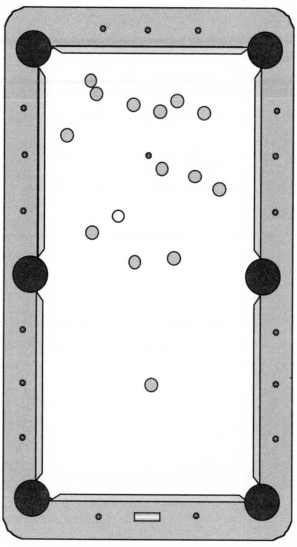

ILLUSTRATION 61

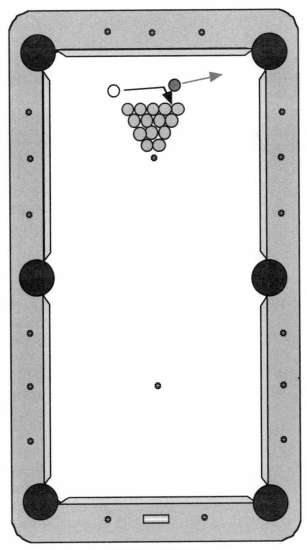

ILLUSTRATION 62

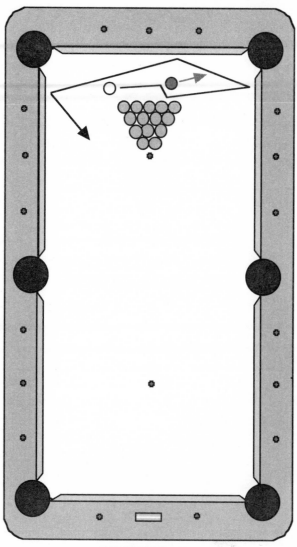

ILLUSTRATION 63

type of focus is important in shots such as the one shown in illustration 62.

When this type of break shot turns out well, you will be left with a layout similar to the one shown in illustration 64. As you can see, fewer balls have broken out from the rack than in our other examples. But there are still plenty of opportunities, and the cue ball has moved off the rack and come to rest in a spot likely to leave you with shots to continue your run.

Practice

Like every other part of this demanding game, developing confidence in hitting break shots requires you to hit lots of them. Repetition and experimentation will allow you to pick up nuances of speed adjustment, stroke (stop stroke, follow, or draw) and english, depending upon variations in how the cue ball and break ball are lying. A good way to do this is to charm (or pay) someone into racking for you so that you can practice a series of break shots without interruption. Second best is to find the patience to rack for yourself, practice the break shot, study the result, rerack the balls right then and there, and then repeat the process.

Don't rely merely on practicing break shots as they come up in a practice run, especially not when you're new to straight pool. The importance of break shots means it's crucial that you become very comfortable executing them. You need to practice them more frequently than once out of every 15 or so shots. As with every other aspect of the game, devoting the most practice time to the types of break shots that you like the least will be your fastest route to improvement.

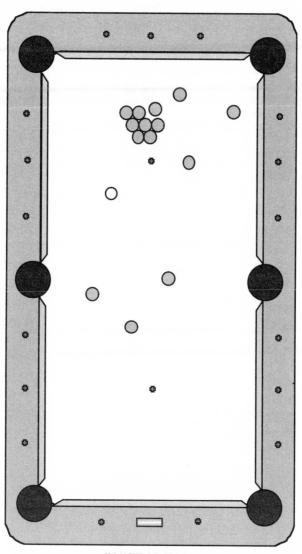

ILLUSTRATION 64

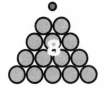

CHAPTER

Safety Play

On occasion, someone who had watched one of my matches would tell me: "You were lucky. You left a shot when you tried to play a safety, and your opponent missed. He should have made the shot." I'd respond by saying: "You're right, he should have made that shot, but I scouted him before the match, and I knew he wouldn't."

One of the keys to high runs is to be the first player with the chance at a shot worth taking. Safety play can give you that chance, forcing your opponent into a miss, a failed safety, or perhaps even a scratch. This is an offense-oriented way to look at safety play.

The flip side, of course, is defense. Generally, you should strive never to miss a called ball. This does *not* mean that you have to become a flawless shot-maker. You must, however, recognize your own shot-making limitations. Taking a 30 percent chance to continue your run with a shot you find dicey gives your opponent a 70 percent chance of coming to the table with a clear shot to start his or her own run. Instead, play safe.

In nine-ball, playing safe involves preventing your opponent from seeing a shot on just one ball, the lowest-numbered ball on the table. (Ideally, a nine-ball safety also involves preventing combinations, caroms, or safeties off the lowest-numbered object ball.) To play a good safety in straight pool, however, you cannot leave a shot on *any* of the balls on the table. In straight pool, after the opening break shot, a legal safety has been played when, after contacting an object ball, the cue ball or any of the object balls touches a rail (or an object ball is pocketed). A successful safety usually involves one of two scenarios. The first is freezing the cue ball against (or as near as possible to) an object ball so that all potential shots are cut off. The second is grazing a ball or cluster of balls as thinly as possible so that all clusters of balls remain intact, leaving no available shots. A good safety pressures the incoming player by giving him or her only two unhappy options: attempting a difficult shot or attempting a difficult safety.

Illustrations 65 and 66 show a safety in which the cue ball freezes against an object ball. Here, the cue ball freezes against the rack, cutting off access to any of the balls loosened from the rack. Illustrations 67 and 68 demonstrate the second type of safety: The cue ball grazes an object ball and rolls up the table. Since the cluster has remained intact, no shots are available to the incoming player.

It would be impossible to describe every conceivable safety situation. Rather than try to do so, I will give you some general principles to keep in mind. It's up to you to apply these general concepts in a creative way when faced with the many and varied situations in which you may decide to play a safety.

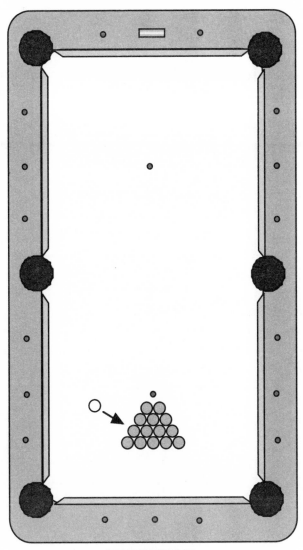

ILLUSTRATION 65

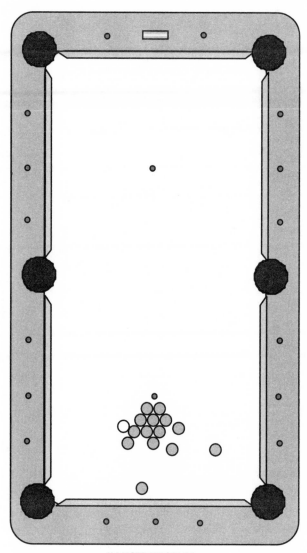

ILLUSTRATION 66

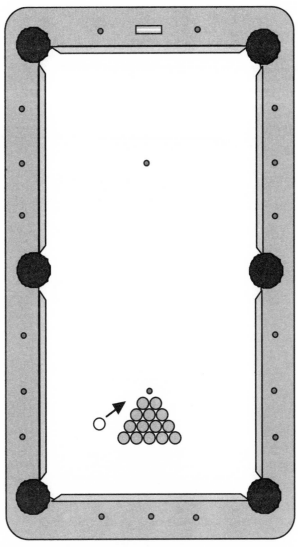

ILLUSTRATION 67

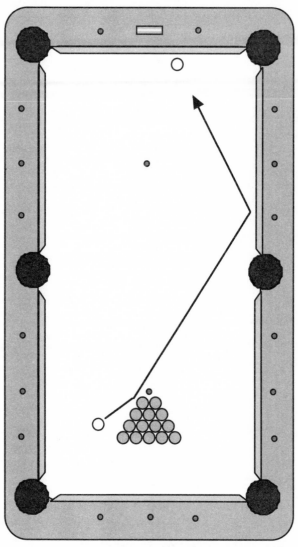

ILLUSTRATION 68

General Concepts

Note that I did not say when you are "forced" to play a safety. You may have a choice between a shot and a safety. What do you do in that situation?

There's no simple answer. You must consider whether, if you play the shot, it's likely that you'll be able to continue your run. If the shot is a dead end (that is, there's no second shot available after you make your first shot), and the safety you can play from the starting position is better than the safety choice you'll have if you first pocket the ball, then play safe now.

There are other factors to consider when deciding to play a safety. They include:

- **Your opponent.** This may be the most critical factor. If you try a shot with some risk and miss, what is the harm likely to be? As the anecdote that opens this chapter shows, I scouted my opponent before a match to find out which shots he liked and which made him uncomfortable. Consider other characteristics of your opponent. Is she left-handed? Does he prefer cut shots to bank shots? Is he short? Is she uncomfortable using a mechanical bridge? Does he have trouble bridging over balls? These little traits mean a lot.
- **Playing conditions.** If the cloth is slow and the air is humid, you can try to freeze the cue ball to an object ball with more confidence. If the cloth is fast, you can get away with a softer hit when trying to graze an object ball and send the cue ball up table, decreasing the risk of either accidentally freeing an object ball that your opponent can

shoot at, or creating a dead (impossible-to-miss) combination shot or carom.

- **The score.** If you are near the end of a close game and neither you nor your opponent is running balls, ball count may be important. This is especially so if making one more ball brings you so much closer to winning that you may not have to get into the next rack—or keeps your opponent from winning unless he or she can execute at least one more break shot.

- **Whether you or your opponent is on a scratch.** Given the three-consecutive-foul rule, if your opponent left the table on a scratch, there's no need for you to execute a legal shot in order to play safe. You can simply roll the cue ball to a spot where your opponent will be faced with limited opportunities. This key factor is often forgotten by a player who has run some balls before considering a safety. Maybe you can get into a superior position by taking a scratch.

- **Whether you have run some balls.** If I've run a fair number of balls, I might deliberately leave my opponent a tough shot and dare him to make it. He's cold by this point so he's likely to miss, which will rattle him even more. If he makes it, it's unlikely he's going to be able to get up and hit me with a good run of his own after sitting down for a while.

Another problem with talking about being "forced" to take a safety is that thinking in that sense about safety play reflects a defeatist attitude. You can win a match with a good safety, and you should consider the chance to play a safety as an opportunity. Don't fall into the trap of carefully constructing a run and then, when things don't go as planned, playing a safety in a hurry, without the same care and attention you would devote to trying to pocket a ball.

Goals in Safety Play

You should strive for certain goals in a safety. As with constructing a run, you must think several sequences ahead. *Never* play a safety merely because it leaves your opponent no shot at his or her next turn at the table. Otherwise, your opponent may be able to play a better safety in response, leaving you in worse shape than you were before you started.

For an example of what I mean, see illustration 69. This shows the table after I have just played a safety. While I did not leave my opponent with an immediate shot, I did leave my opponent with an opportunity to put me on the defensive. As you can see, since I did not loosen any object balls from the cluster when I froze the cue ball against it in illustration 69, my opponent can leave the cue ball anywhere in the vast shaded area shown in illustration 70, and I will be left without a shot.

What makes my safety in illustration 70 particularly ineffective is that my opponent can roll the cue ball *all the way up to the head of the table,* as shown in illustration 71. From there, it will be much more difficult for me to respond with a safety of my own.

When planning your safety, keep the following in mind:

- **Move balls out of clusters.** If you can leave your opponent safe and—at the same time—break free

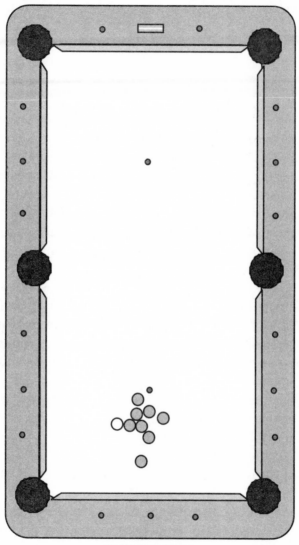

ILLUSTRATION 69

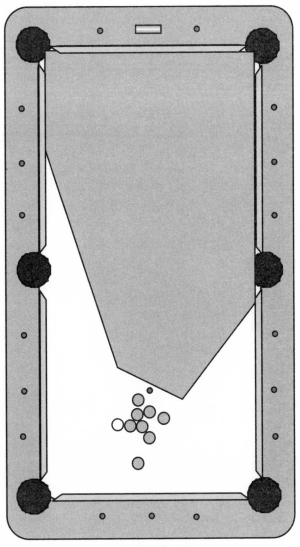

ILLUSTRATION 70

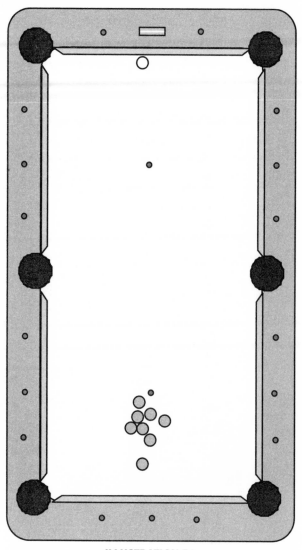

ILLUSTRATION 71

some loose balls, you will greatly diminish the areas on the table from which your opponent can leave you safe in return. In illustration 72 I have played a safety off the same cluster shown in illustration 69. The difference is that I managed to leave my opponent without a shot while hitting the cluster hard enough to jar loose a few balls. My opponent is thus left to try to put me in a much smaller area of the table than was the case in illustration 70. If my opponent now fails to leave me in the very limited shaded area shown in illustration 73, I'll have a shot of some sort.

- **Get to the head of the table.** Play the safety that will allow you to be the first player in a position to play safe while sending the cue ball up table. Playing a safety nearly always requires either a thin cut or a precise hit. Either way, anyone playing a safety from 7 or 8 feet away is at a great disadvantage. Force your opponent to try to play safeties from a distance.

- **Get to a rail.** Like moving balls out of clusters, putting your opponent on the rail greatly limits his or her ability to play a good safety in response. If the cue ball is frozen to a rail, your opponent can only roll the cue ball or follow it, making it hard to try to freeze the cue ball next to an object ball. Also, playing off the rail simply makes any shot more difficult, because english is often accidentally applied. Some of your opponents will make matters worse for themselves by jacking up the rear of their cue on rail shots, adding more risk of applying english.

- **Limit escape routes.** It sounds simplistic—and it is—but remember where the pockets are located. When you freeze the cue ball on an object ball, try

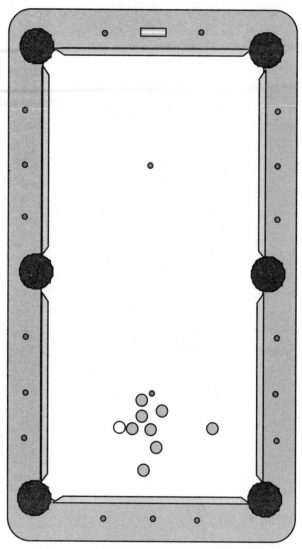

ILLUSTRATION 72

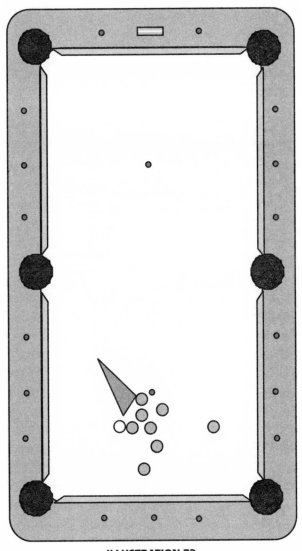

ILLUSTRATION 73

to freeze on a spot that presents a threat of a scratch for your opponent. Illustration 74 shows an example. This is the table layout after I have just played a safety. By freezing the cue ball with the tangent line between it and the adjacent object ball aligned such that the cue ball is headed toward the corner pocket, I've made it difficult for my opponent to avoid a scratch if he or she tries to send the cue ball down table. If my opponent tries to send me up table, I'm likely to be left with a shot.

- **Know where you want to end up.** Before playing your safety, take the time to walk around the table and imagine what your opponent will see once you've shot. You may realize that your plan will leave your opponent a shot or a safety. You might then prefer to pick a different spot for the cue ball to end up on. *Keep this specific location in mind.* Use a reference point so that, after you walk back to the other side of the table, you have a spot picked out for exactly where you want the cue ball to end up. For example, in illustration 75 tell yourself: "Put the cue ball on the rail a diamond and a half from the side pocket." Be precise.

Taking a Foul

The goals outlined above also apply to situations in which you are deliberately taking a foul because your opponent is already on a scratch (that is, your opponent has scratched to end his or her last turn at the table—and you did not scratch on your last turn). Obviously, it will be easier to accomplish one or more of

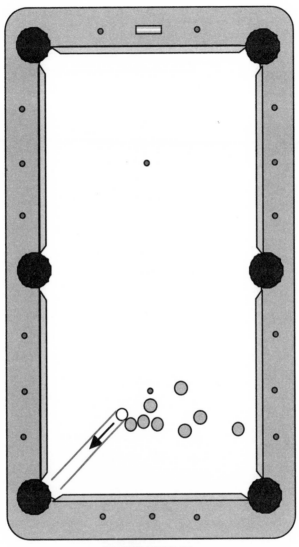

ILLUSTRATION 74

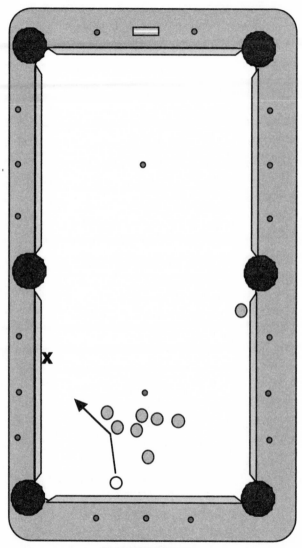

ILLUSTRATION 75

I had better get from where I am now (the foot rail) to the *precise* location marked X by the side rail. Otherwise, I'm likely to leave my opponent a shot.

these goals when you are taking a scratch (as opposed to a typical safety), because you'll be relieved of the need to meet the requirements for a legal shot. For this reason, when your opponent is on a scratch and you can play a safety by taking a scratch yourself, you enjoy a tremendous opportunity to take control of the game.

Deliberately taking a foul when your opponent is *not* on a scratch is generally considered a sophisticated move, and rightly so. Like pushing out after the break in nine-ball, you're essentially betting that you know something your opponent doesn't.

Let's say that you are left in a tough position. Neither you nor your opponent is on a scratch, and he or she executes a legal safety, leaving you in the ugly situation presented in illustration 76. What do you do?

Employ a two-step response. Step one is to take a deliberate scratch, nudging the cue ball so that the tangent line is perpendicular to a rail (in this case the foot rail). See illustration 77. Your opponent will often do nothing more than take a deliberate scratch in return, touching the cue ball but leaving it where it is for fear of moving something in a way that will leave you a shot. The strategy of your opponent is to force you to scratch three times in a row before he or she does.

Now, step two: You graze object ball X with left english, as shown in illustration 78. The cue ball will go to the rail, back, and hug the bottom of the rack, ending up as shown in the illustration. This is not difficult to execute. Recognizing situations when this strategy (or an adaptation) can be effective is the key.

What do you do if your *opponent* takes a deliberate scratch? One possibility is that your opponent has moved the cue ball so that a shot opportunity now exists

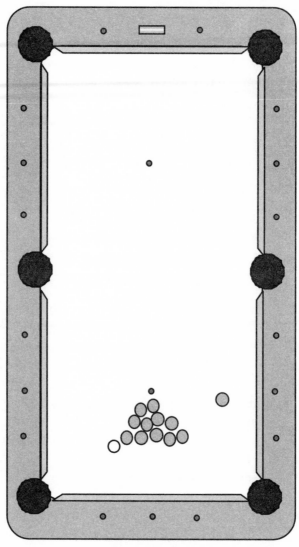

ILLUSTRATION 76

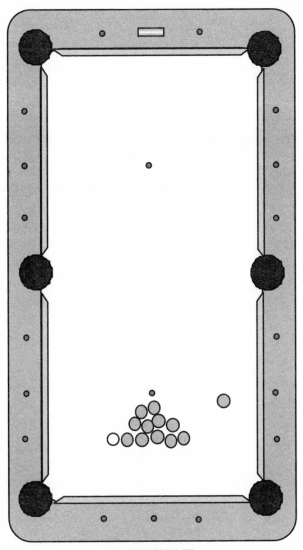

ILLUSTRATION 77

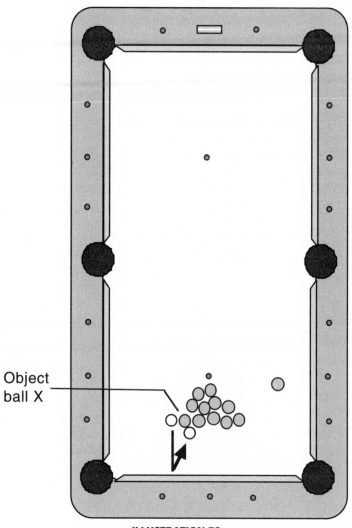

Object
ball X

ILLUSTRATION 78

that was not available before; survey the table for that potential opportunity. It's more likely that your opponent is pushing the cue ball to a spot from which a safety can be played. You may be able to figure out what your opponent has in mind and respond accordingly. If not, you can simply push the cue ball back to its original position, making sure that no object balls have been moved in such a way as to create a shot or safety that was not available before.

One of the many beautiful aspects of billiards is that it allows different players to express themselves according to their individual personalities. I was always an offense-minded player. I wanted to run balls and outdistance my opponent. Other, more defense-minded players became effective by taking very few risks and becoming expert at identifying and executing devastating safeties. These defense-minded players tied up their opponents and defeated them without necessarily running high numbers during their own innings at the table. Obviously, the most successful player is the one who can do it all, putting pressure on the opponent based on the offensive threat of a long run, and combining that threat with the ability to seal off any potential shots when the occasion calls for safety play. No matter what your own style happens to be, to play the game at a high level you must become proficient at playing safeties.

Bank Shots in Straight Pool

When I was playing on 5- by 10-foot tables, most of the experienced players would say: "If you're in bad-enough position to be thinking about playing a bank, you're in good-enough position to play a safety."

Some players today, even on the current regulation-size tables (4½ by 9 feet), never play a bank in a straight pool game, because they think it's too risky. I am not one of those players. For one thing, some banks are easy relative to a long nonbank shot. These easier banks generally consist of shots where the object ball is close to a side rail and can be made by banking the ball across the width of the table. See illustration 79. Another example is where there's an object ball close to the intended pocket—so that a banked ball will carom into the pocket even if your bank shot would otherwise be slightly off target. See illustration 80.

147

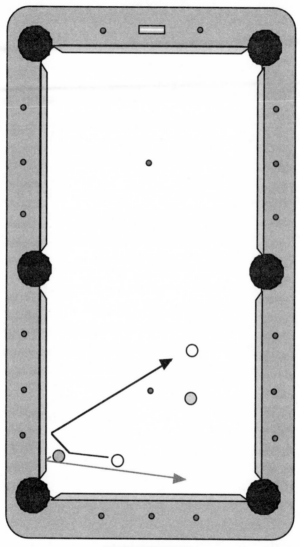

ILLUSTRATION 79

Also, there are times when your options are limited. It may be late in a particular rack where there are no reasonable safety options. In those cases—where you're unlikely to leave your opponent safe whether you try a safety *or* a bank—you might as well play the bank and at least give yourself a chance to continue your run.

Generally, however, I won't risk a bank shot unless I'm behind by a wide margin and need to put together a good run to have any chance to win the match, or I'm on a good run. The first situation is self-explanatory. In the second situation my rationale is that, since I'm in the middle of a solid run, I'm obviously in stroke and have good feel for the characteristics of the table. In either case I've got to rely on memory.

As I noted in chapter 1, Equipment, all tables play differently, as will different parts of the same table. This is especially true with the rails, which is why I make a point of hitting banks on *each* rail of a table *before* starting an important match or event.

If you're going to play a bank shot, play position off the shot. Don't settle for merely pocketing the ball. Otherwise, you've given yourself the worst of all possible worlds: You're starting off by playing a lower-percentage shot; you're leaving position to chance, such that—if you make the bank—you may not be able to continue your run; and if you miss, you're likely to leave your opponent a shot on the ball you were trying to pocket (if not some other object ball). For these reasons, once you decide to play a bank, play it with verve! Don't play the shot timidly. If you've decided that a bank shot is the correct shot, give yourself the best chance to make the ball by hitting the bank at a medium speed. Do not underhit the bank, which leads to less predictable angles.

Although you should play position off your bank shots, *you need not complicate matters* in your effort to do so.

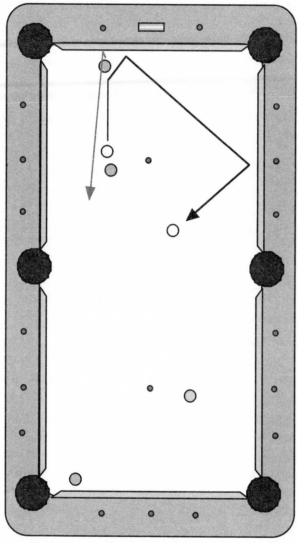

ILLUSTRATION 80

You can get a lot done with just stop, follow, and draw. Naturally, this is true when playing position off any type of shot. With bank shots especially, however, adding english throws another variable into the mix, which will make pocketing the ball that much more complicated.

Two drills are shown in illustrations 81 and 82. The first helps you develop a sense for the angles and touch needed to pocket banks. In this drill, take the cue ball in hand after each bank, and work from the center of the table toward the end rail. The point is to pocket the bank and observe where the object ball must hit the rail in order to be directed into the opposite side pocket. Theories, schemes, and systems abound on the subject of where to hit a bank shot. This drill, however, will teach you more about where to hit a bank shot (in general, and on the table you're using at the time) than any rule of thumb or elaborate diagram. Remember to hit your banks hard enough to get a consistent bounce off the rail.

The second drill is a position drill. It's set up as shown in illustration 82, with the object balls lined up along the sides of the table, roughly a ball's width from the side rail. There's no ball in hand on this one, but you can play the balls in any order. The object is to successfully bank each of the balls along the rails in such a way that you can obtain position for your next bank shot. As you gain confidence, add balls to this drill. There's no use trying this second drill until you are very comfortable altering speeds to vary the bounce—stroking more softly to widen angles, and more firmly to shorten them. This drill will also teach you how to pocket banks where the cue ball crosses over the object ball. An example of this type of bank shot is shown in illustration 83. When practicing this drill, you will find that you achieve the greatest success by keeping the cue ball well off the rails after each shot. See illustration 84.

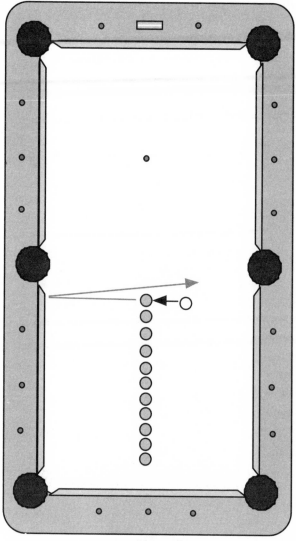

ILLUSTRATION 81

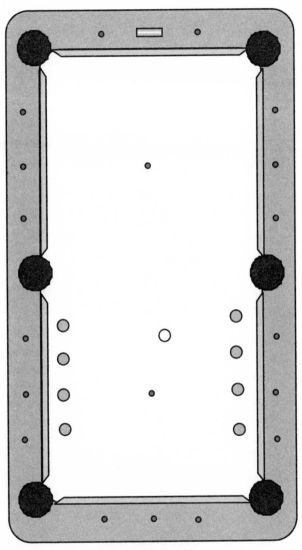

ILLUSTRATION 82

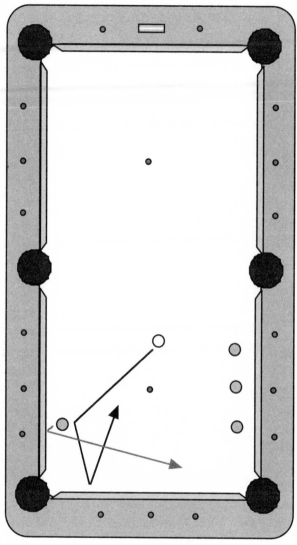

ILLUSTRATION 83

An example of a crossover bank shot.

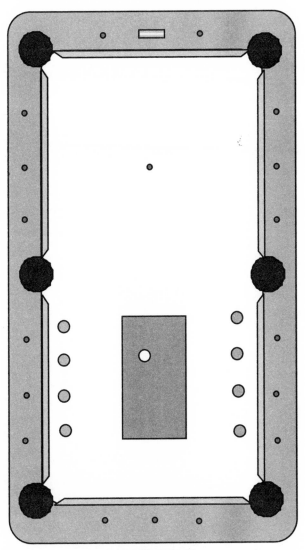

ILLUSTRATION 84

Try to keep the cue ball in the area of the table covered by the shaded rectangle after each bank shot. This will allow you the most position options for getting shape on your next bank.

CHAPTER 10

Mental Approach

I've long admired Jimmy Caras. He was a gutsy player who always played his game. He may not have been as naturally talented as Willie Mosconi, but when it mattered, Caras would reel him in, finding a way—through his mental toughness—to win with the talents he did possess.

Throughout the previous chapters, I've discussed mental approach to some degree, by guiding you on how to think your way through a straight pool game. This chapter provides a closer look at the important role of what may be more accurately called mental attitude.

Developing Touch

Watch any professional-caliber player and you will notice that he or she has a sense of feel for the cue ball, the object balls, and the table—how the tip feels on the cue ball at impact, the sound of the cue ball making contact with the object ball (different depending on whether the cue ball is making a full hit on the object ball or merely grazing it), the speed of the balls, how far the clustered object balls will spread on impact, how much of the cue ball's speed will be absorbed by a rail, and so forth. This is true whether the player employs a gentle style or a more authoritative one.

The first step toward developing this type of touch in your own game is to try to remain as observant and aware as possible. Take the trouble to notice how the cue ball feels at impact with your cue, and how that sensation differs depending on the speed of the stroke and where you are contacting the cue ball. Make sure the fundamentals of your stroke production are sound. You will not be able to distinguish fine differences in the feel of the hit if you are gripping the cue stick too tightly or too far back with your rear hand.

Although it sounds odd, you should also try to develop a feel for objects that you don't even touch. For instance, observe, think about, and calibrate how the way in which you stroke the cue ball affects the impact between the cue ball and the object ball. Develop this sense of feel with every type of shot and safety you play, whenever you play. By developing this sense of touch and thinking about it as you visualize your next shot or safety, you will learn to pocket balls, achieve position, and execute safeties that would be virtually impossible otherwise.

Confidence

Closely related to touch is a sense of confidence. Developing the feeling of complete awareness that translates into touch goes a long way toward creating confidence.

You should do more than merely visualize yourself pocketing the object ball. You should *know* the following with each shot:

- If you deliver the cue ball to the proper point, the object ball *must* go in.
- You *are* aiming at the proper point.
- Your stroke *will* deliver the cue ball to the point of aim.

At the moment you are prepared to stroke the cue ball, all of this should be in place. If not, get out of your stance and start from the beginning—visualizing the aiming point and looking at the shot from the straight-in perspective. In this way you will shoot only when you are absolutely ready, and you will have complete confidence in each shot by the time you are actually executing it.

Some players have so much confidence in their games that they look shocked (or indignant) when they miss a shot after successfully running a number of balls. These players believe—as you must, if you are going to progress in this game—that they have done everything properly in terms of preparing to execute the shot. This positive mental attitude is part of what enables all successful players to put together runs.

Overcoming Mental Barriers

Perhaps you are at the stage where you are running a fair number of balls—in the 20s, 30s, 40s, or beyond—but find it difficult to reach the next level of proficiency. Often, when a player approaches his or her high run, the run somehow comes to an end.

Before I ran 100 for the first time, I had put together many runs in the 80s and 90s. I came very close to running 100 a number of times before I finally broke that barrier. As soon as I'd reached 100 the first time, it became much easier to run past 100. That mark ceased to be a barrier for me.

To overcome such a barrier, it helps to stop thinking about ball count and focus on frames. Once you are thinking in terms of frames (or racks) of 14, the numbers (25, 50, 100 . . .) start to lose their power over you.

If you are at the stage where running 5 balls, 10 balls, or a rack is a good run, it still helps to think in terms of the frame: identifying and creating break balls and key balls, recognizing and attacking problems, and all the other aspects discussed in chapter 6, Managing the Frame. By doing so, you begin to think in terms of problem-solving and the task at hand, and not in terms of any artificial limits on your abilities.

In short, you are playing the table, not the opponent or yourself. This mental approach should help you overcome barriers such as surpassing your high-run number, defeating an opponent who has always given you trouble, or mastering a particular situation (for example, winning a tournament or getting beyond a certain round in a tournament). It has worked for me.

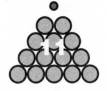

Competing

Competition has nearly always been a part of my life. Since I was a child—10 years old or so—I have been playing tournaments and exhibition matches. The tournaments had a pressure all their own. I have won a number of titles against some pretty strong fields, and I've lost my share, too. Competing in the exhibition matches was also interesting in its own way. There I had a chance to match up against some of the champions of the day, including Willie Hoppe, Ralph Greenleaf, Ruth McGinnis, and Irwin Rudolph. During one period, it was popular for players who called themselves the "Masked Marvel" (or similar names) to tour from room to room and take on all comers. I had the chance to play against some of these Masked Marvels, and I beat several of them when I was still 12 and 13 years old.

As I got older, I continued to compete at pool but playing basketball, golf, bowling, and—most significantly—working took time away from my pool game. From the time I was a young adult, I always worked full time, whether it was on my family's farm or at a job (including working as a vice president selling Muzak to offices, restaurants, and the like for 40 years). Obviously, this limited my ability to focus on pool. I remember the way Marge Caras, Jimmy Caras's wife, used to tease my wife, Ruth. Marge would say that she was angry with me for showing up at tournaments here and there, and knocking out pros (like Jimmy) who were playing in *every* tournament and devoting 100 percent of their lives to the game.

I learned that even if you are not be able to devote as much time to your pool game as you'd like, there are ways you can bring out the best in your abilities during competition. An important technique is to *constantly* study the table. Even when the other guy is shooting, study the table after the break and plan your attack on the layout. Don't wait until your turn comes up and arrive at the table cold. One of the most devastating—and unique—qualities of this game is that, by succeeding during your own innings, you can deprive your opponent of opportunities to even *attempt* to score. When you're the one stuck in the chair, consider yourself an active part of the game. This will minimize the advantage your opponent gains during his or her runs.

It also helps to think of billiards as a sport and prepare for competition, mentally and physically, with that attitude. I don't compete anymore, but now that I am in my 80s, it's amazing for me to look back and see how much I learned from my father about playing competitively. One of the things he taught me was to train for billiards like a sport. To the extent that I have succeeded at competing, from the junior level up to the World's Professional title level, part of the reason was my training and preparation. Although I did not always compete regularly (as Marge Caras noticed), I often played well when I did compete. That came from training for any upcoming event.

My father used to have me run. I'd run 3 miles at least four mornings a week. I eventually began to enjoy it, but I probably didn't understand the importance of maintaining good physical condition as much as he did. He was always a good athlete and used to tell me that the running would help carry me through a tournament, where I might have to play as many as three long matches a day. The running also gave me the stamina to practice longer.

Part of training for any regimen is to structure your diet. Besides running, I tried to pay attention to what I was eating. Before a match, I didn't want to get weighted down with a heavy meal. At all times, I tried to eat a well-balanced diet and to eat enough so that my energy level could remain high throughout the time I was practicing or playing my matches.

I even made a point of trying to save my eyesight by avoiding reading too much if I had a tourney coming up. I didn't take this idea as far as some others, though. When I was about 17, I was sent by Brunswick to drive Willie Hoppe around as he gave exhibitions. The idea was that I'd learn how to give an entertaining exhibition myself, a skill Hoppe was definitely qualified to teach. In order to save himself for his matches and shows, however, Hoppe never ran on his own errands, made arrangements, or carried any of his own bags, cases, or other gear when I was traveling with him. According to

Hoppe, that was *my* job. Hoppe was never too stressed to play well, but I was getting run ragged. (I eventually quit. I told him that I'd been hired to drive him, not be his slave.)

In terms of preparation on the table, you should put in enough practice time to accustom yourself to maintaining your concentration and stamina in match after match. Don't overdo it, however. I'd try to practice at least 2½ to 3 hours a day before a competition. For me, I found that if I practiced for too long at a stretch, I'd get stale. Your own makeup will, of course, be different. Be sensitive to how many quality hours of practice you are able to put in before you start to lose focus.

My aim was to make the most of my practice time and to keep my concentration level high during the entire session. As Hogan taught, I practiced whatever shots were giving me trouble. I made sure I practiced longer shots, such as spot shots and at least some bank shots. I played these shots over and over, but each time I'd give myself a different position target for the cue ball. I moved from table to table so that I wasn't subconsciously relying on my familiarity with any particular table.

If you are about to play a tournament and can get to the site of the competition early for a practice session or two, do so. I would have loved to have been able to travel to tournament sites early enough to practice on the same equipment and under the same conditions where my matches would be played, but I generally couldn't afford the time to do so.

Where there's competition at pool, there is—at least sometimes—gambling. Although not nearly as prevalent as in years past, you will always find some pool players who gamble. There's much debate over whether gambling helps or hinders your ability to compete in tournaments. Like every pool player of my era, I sometimes gambled outside of tournaments, but I never felt that tournament play involved an ounce less pressure than playing for money. Every now and then, however, I'd overhear some smart spectator say, "He'd never have made that shot if he had been gambling." What those types of people did not understand was that, in a tournament situation, I was playing for my life with every match. If I lost $50 on a money match, I could always try to win it back. That's not the case when it's your pride at stake. I felt much worse losing a tournament match than a gambling match because there was no second chance.

Although hardened gamblers tended to look down on professional players, they weren't always anxious to match up. One time, after I had given an exhibition, one of the fellows watching walked up to me and announced that he wanted to play me a $500 game the next day. I had no idea who the guy was, but I figured that if he was someone to worry about, I would have heard of him. I showed up the next day and asked if he was ready to play. His reply was brief: "I slept it off."

Whether or not you gamble or play tournaments, the point of improving your game should transcend simply winning money. While it is possible to earn some money playing pool, every professional player will tell you that there are many better ways to make money than through this game. When I was looking to put my boys through college in the early 1960s, the movie *The Hustler* had recently been released, and pool was enjoying enhanced popularity. This meant more prize money for tournaments, so I got out my cue and started competing again so that my wife and I could more easily send our sons to school. While there were more financial rewards in pool for a while, that boom did not last.

Pool offers other rewards, though. Unlike bowlers, who face the same frame time and time again, billiards presents endless variety. After the balls are broken, every single rack will be different. The game will force you to think and be creative on your feet.

Creativity alone is not enough, however. Succeeding at billiards also requires raw memorization. It will at all times be critical that you remember shots, patterns, and pitfalls from past games, because the same or similar situations will recur.

All of these challenges offer the chance to improve, to earn a sense of accomplishment, and to appreciate the many beautiful aspects of the game. The richest rewards pool has to offer can be gained by anyone. You do not need to be a champion at billiards to benefit from the game. I hope that, with whatever additional understanding this book has been able to provide, you will enjoy those rewards with ever greater frequency.

CHAPTER

Acknowledgments

Special thanks to Mike Shamos for his interest in this project, his support, and his practical advice. Were it not for him, this book might not have seen the light of day. Thanks also to everyone who has contributed to our effort to present this material or has otherwise stood by us over the years, including our families; our editor, Enrica Gadler; Jeremy Goldsmith; John "J. J." Juback; Arnold Silvernail; Karen Hetz; and Mitchell Kaufman.

CHAPTER

About the Authors

Arthur "Babe" Cranfield

Born on September 24, 1915, to Arthur Sr. and Isabel Cranfield, Babe lived, at various times, in the New York City borough of the Bronx; Hudson, New York, where his family operated a farm; and Syracuse, New York, where he lives today.

During much of Babe's childhood, his father owned and ran a poolroom, although its locale changed as Babe's family moved from place to place. Thus, Babe was exposed to billiards from an early age and could practice for free, advantages that combined with his natural gifts to produce an unusual talent. By the time he was 12, Babe could run 100 balls at straight pool. He also excelled as a youth in many other sports, including basketball, tennis, baseball, bowling, and golf, in which he captured a number of titles, for a while considering playing golf as a career.

In the 1930s Babe attended Cornell University in Ithaca, New York, intending to study agricultural techniques to benefit his family's farm. His time at college was cut short, however, when he accepted an offer to tour the country performing billiards exhibitions promoted by Sylvester Livingston, who managed tours for most of the prominent billiards stars of that era.

Babe enjoys the distinction of being the only billiards player in history to have won the premier titles at every available level of play. In addition to many others, Babe won the United States Junior Championship when he was 15 years old; the U.S. Amateur Championship three consecutive times (in 1938, 1939, and 1940); and the World's Professional Championship in 1964. He captured the World's Professional title in a challenge match over the then–world title holder, Luther Lassiter. Contested in a multiday "block" format, Babe prevailed by a final score of 1,200 to 730.

In recognition of his achievements, on July 19, 1997, the Billiard Congress of America inducted Babe into its Hall of Fame. Babe is also a member of the Syracuse Sports Hall of Fame.

Outside of pool, Babe made his mark by serving in the air force during World War II, and, later, joining Background Music, Inc., a major distributor for Muzak, after short stints in other jobs. Babe advanced to the position of vice president of sales within that company, where his career ultimately spanned 40 years.

In December 1940 Babe married Ruth Fish. Together they raised two sons, Lawrence and Gary, and now have four grandchildren, Zachary, John, David, and Kelly. Today Babe and Ruth live in the same house in Syracuse that they have called home since 1945. While both have been retired for some time, Babe still plays billiards occasionally and Ruth remains active in volunteer work, particularly with youth bowling organizations.

Laurence S. Moy

Born in 1960 in Plainfield, New Jersey, to Jack and Mary Moy, Larry grew up with his sister, Taryn, in Astoria, Queens (New York), and later in Rockland County, New York. Larry first saw pocket billiards played in a poolroom next door to his parents' Chinese restaurant in Nanuet, New York. He remembers marveling at how the players he watched could somehow make the cue ball move from one end of the table to the other for position on their next shot. Larry did not start playing regularly until 1978, when he was 18 years old. That same year, he began attending Cornell University in Ithaca, where he first saw Babe Cranfield perform an exhibition.

At Cornell, Larry won the university championship and other titles numerous times. Perhaps his biggest achievement, however, was graduating with a bachelor's degree in four years (a feat many of the dedicated pool players on campus took somewhat longer to accomplish). In 1982 Larry began law school, also at Cornell, not touching a cue once in his first year of legal study but returning to the game to win the ACU-I intercollegiate title in 1985 for the region covering New York and Canada. (Although this win qualified Larry to compete in the national ACU-I tournament, no such tournament was held in 1985 due to lack of a sponsor.)

Larry now lives with his wife, Karen, and two children, Christopher and Hannah, near New York City, where he is a partner with a law firm specializing in litigation and employment law. In addition to pool, Larry has maintained a strong interest in music (having played piano and guitar from an early age), basketball, and racquet sports (tennis, squash, and table tennis).

The highlight of Larry's pool life was being invited by the Billiard Congress of America to make the presentation for induction of Babe Cranfield into the BCA Hall of Fame in July 1997.